G000098450

IMAGE EVALUATION
TEST TARGET (MT-3)

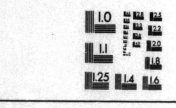

|← 6" →|

Photographic
Sciences
Corporation

23 WEST MAIN STREET
WEBSTER, N.Y. 14580
(716) 872-4503

**CIHM/ICMH
Microfiche
Series.**

**CIHM/ICMH
Collection de
microfiches.**

Canadian Institute for Historical Microreproductions / Institut canadien de microreproductions historiques

© 1985

Technical and Bibliographic Notes/Notes techniques et bibliographiques

The Institute has attempted to obtain the best original copy available for filming. Features of this copy which may be bibliographically unique, which may alter any of the images in the reproduction, or which may significantly change the usual method of filming, are checked below.

L'Institut a microfilmé le meilleur exemplaire qu'il lui a été possible de se procurer. Les détails de cet exemplaire qui sont peut-être uniques du point de vue bibliographique, qui peuvent modifier une image reproduite, ou qui peuvent exiger une modification dans la méthode normale de filmage sont indiqués ci-dessous.

- [ ] Coloured covers/
  Couverture de couleur

- [ ] Covers damaged/
  Couverture endommagée

- [ ] Covers restored and/or laminated/
  Couverture restaurée et/ou pelliculée

- [ ] Cover title missing/
  Le titre de couverture manque

- [ ] Coloured maps/
  Cartes géographiques en couleur

- [ ] Coloured ink (i.e. other than blue or black)/
  Encre de couleur (i.e. autre que bleue ou noire)

- [ ] Coloured plates and/or illustrations/
  Planches et/ou illustrations en couleur

- [ ] Bound with other material/
  Relié avec d'autres documents

- [ ] Tight binding may cause shadows or distortion along interior margin/
  La reliure serrée peut causer de l'ombre ou de la distortion le long de la marge intérieure

- [ ] Blank leaves added during restoration may appear within the text. Whenever possible, these have been omitted from filming/
  Il se peut que certaines pages blanches ajoutées lors d'une restauration apparaissent dans le texte, mais, lorsque cela était possible, ces pages n'ont pas été filmées.

- [ ] Additional comments:/
  Commentaires supplémentaires:

- [ ] Coloured pages/
  Pages de couleur

- [ ] Pages damaged/
  Pages endommagées

- [ ] Pages restored and/or laminated/
  Pages restaurées et/ou pelliculées

- [x] Pages discoloured, stained or foxed/
  Pages décolorées, tachetées ou piquées

- [ ] Pages detached/
  Pages détachées

- [x] Showthrough/
  Transparence

- [ ] Quality of print varies/
  Qualité inégale de l'impression

- [ ] Includes supplementary material/
  Comprend du matériel supplémentaire

- [ ] Only edition available/
  Seule édition disponible

- [ ] Pages wholly or partially obscured by errata slips, tissues, etc., have been refilmed to ensure the best possible image/
  Les pages totalement ou partiellement obscurcies par un feuillet d'errata, une pelure, etc., ont été filmées à nouveau de façon à obtenir la meilleure image possible.

This item is filmed at the reduction ratio checked below/
Ce document est filmé au taux de réduction indiqué ci-dessous.

10X		14X			18X			22X			26X			30X		
			✓													
	12X			16X			20X			24X			28X			32X

The copy filmed here has been reproduced thanks to the generosity of:

National Library of Canada

The images appearing here are the best quality possible considering the condition and legibility of the original copy and in keeping with the filming contract specifications.

Original copies in printed paper covers are filmed beginning with the front cover and ending on the last page with a printed or illustrated impression, or the back cover when appropriate. All other original copies are filmed beginning on the first page with a printed or illustrated impression, and ending on the last page with a printed or illustrated impression.

The last recorded frame on each microfiche shall contain the symbol →(meaning "CONTINUED"), or the symbol ▽ (meaning "END"), whichever applies.

Maps, plates, charts, etc., may be filmed at different reduction ratios. Those too large to be entirely included in one exposure are filmed beginning in the upper left hand corner, left to right and top to bottom, as many frames as required. The following diagrams illustrate the method:

L'exemplaire filmé fut reproduit grâce à la générosité de:

Bibliothèque nationale du Canada

Les images suivantes ont été reproduites avec le plus grand soin, compte tenu de la condition et de la netteté de l'exemplaire filmé, et en conformité avec les conditions du contrat de filmage.

Les exemplaires originaux dont la couverture en papier est imprimée sont filmés en commençant par le premier plat et en terminant soit par la dernière page qui comporte une empreinte d'impression ou d'illustration, soit par le second plat, selon le cas. Tous les autres exemplaires originaux sont filmés en commençant par la première page qui comporte une empreinte d'impression ou d'illustration et en terminant par la dernière page qui comporte une telle empreinte.

Un des symboles suivants apparaîtra sur la dernière image de chaque microfiche, selon le cas: le symbole → signifie "A SUIVRE", le symbole ▽ signifie "FIN".

Les cartes, planches, tableaux, etc., peuvent être filmés à des taux de réduction différents. Lorsque le document est trop grand pour être reproduit en un seul cliché, il est filmé à partir de l'angle supérieur gauche, de gauche à droite, et de haut en bas, en prenant le nombre d'images nécessaire. Les diagrammes suivants illustrent la méthode.

Rm. 27

Mofry Chrailer,

Bro. Webb.

THE PROPERTY OF
THE
LIBRARY OF PARLIAMENT

Listed £200 of ~~Presbyterian Church in Canada. General Assembly~~ T⁵⁷.

THE

PRESBYTERIAN HYMN BOOK

COMPILED BY

A COMMITTEE OF THE GENERAL ASSEMBLY

OF

THE PRESBYTERIAN CHURCH

IN CANADA.

JAMES CAMPBELL AND SON.

TORONTO.

1880.

BV430
P76
1880

Entered, according to the Act of the Parliament of Canada, in the year Eighteen Hundred and Eighty, by the Rev. JOHN JENKINS, D.D., LL.D., and the Rev. WILLIAM GREGG, D.D., in the office of the Minister of Agriculture.

CONTENTS.

I.— GOD: HIS ATTRIBUTES AND WORKS.

1   P. M.

" They rest not day and night, saying, Holy, holy, holy, Lord God Almighty."

1. HOLY, holy, holy, Lord God Almighty!
      Early in the morning our song shall rise to
         Thee;
   Holy, holy, holy, merciful and mighty,
      God in Three Persons, blessèd Trinity!

2. Holy, holy, holy! all the saints adore Thee,
      Casting down their golden crowns around the
         glassy sea;
   Cherubim and seraphim falling down before
         Thee,
      Which wert, and art, and evermore shalt be.

3. Holy, holy, holy! though the darkness hide
         Thee,
      Though the eye of sinful man Thy glory may
         not see;
   Only Thou art holy; there is none beside Thee
      Perfect in power, in love, and purity.

4. Holy, holy, holy, Lord God Almighty!
      All Thy works shall praise Thy name, in earth
         and sky and sea;
   Holy, holy, holy, merciful and mighty,
      God in Three Persons, blessèd Trinity!

I

2 7s.

"Holy, holy, holy, is the Lord of hosts."

1. HOLY, holy, holy Lord
   God of hosts! when heaven and earth
Out of darkness, at Thy word,
   Issued into glorious birth,
All Thy works before Thee stood,
And Thine eye beheld them good,
While they sang, with sweet accord,
Holy, holy, holy Lord!

2. Holy, holy, holy! Thee,
   One Jehovah evermore,
Father, Son, and Spirit! we,
   Dust and ashes, would adore;
Lightly by the world esteemed,
From that world by Thee redeemed,
Sing we here, with glad accord,
Holy, holy, holy Lord!

3. Holy, holy, holy! All
   Heaven's triumphant choir shall sing,
When the ransomed nations fall
   At the footstool of their King;
Then shall saints and seraphim,
Hearts and voices, swell one hymn,
Round the Throne with full accord,
Holy, holy, holy Lord!

3 6, 8.

*"Unto the King eternal, immortal,
invisible, the only wise God, be
honour and glory for ever and
ever."*

1. WE give immortal praise
      To God the Father's love,
   For all our comforts here
      And better hopes above;

He sent His own eternal Son
To die for sins that man had done.

2.   To God the Son belongs
      Immortal glory too,
  Who bought us with His blood
      From everlasting woe;
And now He lives, and now He reigns,
And sees the fruit of all His pains.

3.   To God the Spirit's name
      Immortal worship give,
  Whose new-creating power
      Makes the dead sinner live;
His work completes the great design,
And fills the soul with joy divine.

4.   Almighty God, to Thee
      Be endless honours done,
  The undivided Three,
      And the mysterious One!
Where reason fails with all her powers,
There faith prevails, and love adores.

4   L. M.

"The grace of the Lord Jesus Christ, and
the love of God, and the communion of
the Holy Ghost."

1. FATHER of heaven, whose love profound
A ransom for our souls hath found,
Before Thy throne we sinners bend,
To us Thy pardoning love extend.

2. Almighty Son, Incarnate Word,
Our Prophet, Priest, Redeemer, Lord;
Before Thy throne we sinners bend,
To us Thy saving grace extend.

3

3. Eternal Spirit, by whose breath
   The soul is raised from sin and death;
   Before Thy throne we sinners bend,
   To us Thy quickening power extend.

4. Thrice holy! Father, Spirit, Son;
   Mysterious Godhead, Three in One;
   Before Thy throne we sinners bend,
   Grace, pardon, life, to us extend.

5   8, 7.

" Thou shalt guide me with thy counsel, and
afterward receive me to glory."

1. LEAD us, heavenly Father, lead us
   O'er the world's tempestuous sea;
   Guard us, guide us, keep us, feed us,
   For we have no help but Thee;
   Yet possessing every blessing,
   If our God our Father be.

2. Saviour, breathe forgiveness o'er us;
   All our weakness Thou dost know;
   Thou didst tread this earth before us,
   Thou didst feel its keenest woe;
   Lone and dreary, faint and weary,
   Through the desert Thou didst go.

3. Spirit of our God, descending,
   Fill our hearts with heavenly joy;
   Love with every passion blending,
   Pleasure that can never cloy;
   Thus provided, pardoned, guided,
   Nothing can our peace destroy.

4

8, 7, 4.

*" Blessing, and honour, and glory, and
power be unto him that sitteth upon
the throne, and unto the Lamb for
ever and ever."*

1. GLORY be to God the Father,
    Glory be to God the Son,
Glory be to God the Spirit,
    Great Jehovah, Three in One;
        Glory, glory,
    While eternal ages run!

2. Glory be to Him who loved us,
    Washed us from each spot and stain;
Glory be to Him who bought us,
    Made us kings with Him to reign;
        Glory, glory,
    To the Lamb that once was slain!

3. Glory to the King of angels,
    Glory to the Church's King,
Glory to the King of nations,
    Heaven and earth your praises bring;
        Glory, glory,
    To the King of glory bring!

4. Glory, blessing, praise eternal!
    Thus the choir of angels sings;
Honour, riches, power, dominion!
    Thus its praise creation brings;
        Glory, glory,
    Glory to the King of kings!

7   L. M.

*" Sing unto the Lord a new song, and
his praise in the congregation of
saints."*

1. THEE God we praise, Thee Lord confess,
    Thee, Father everlasting, bless;

The tribes of earth and air and sea
With wondrous voices worship Thee.

2. To Thee all angels ceaseless cry,
   With all the princes of the sky;
   The cherub and the seraph join,
   And thus they hymn the praise divine:

3. Thee, holy, holy, holy King,
   Lord of Sabaoth, Thee we sing;
   Both heaven and earth are full of Thee,
   Father of boundless majesty.

4. Thee, the apostles' glorious choir,
   Thee, prophets with their tongues of fire,
   Thee, white-robed hosts of martyrs bright,
   All serve and praise by day and night.

5. Thee, through the earth, Thy saints confess,
   Thee, Father infinite, they bless,
   Thee, true, divine, and only Son,
   Thee, Holy Spirit, Three in One.

8   L. M.

*" Make a joyful noise unto the Lord, all
ye lands."*

1. BEFORE Jehovah's awful throne,
   Ye nations, bow with sacred joy;
   Know that the Lord is God alone,
   He can create, and He destroy.

2. His sovereign power, without our aid,
   Made us of clay, and formed us men;
   And, when like wandering sheep we strayed,
   He brought us to His fold again.

6

3. We'll crowd Thy gates with thankful songs,
    High as the heavens our voices raise;
And earth, with her ten thousand tongues,
    Shall fill Thy courts with sounding praise.

4. Wide as the world is Thy command,
    Vast as eternity Thy love;
Firm as a rock Thy truth must stand,
    When rolling years shall cease to move.

9   L. M.

" The Lord reigneth, let the earth rejoice."

1. THE Lord is King! lift up thy voice,
    O earth, and, all ye heavens, rejoice!
From world to world the joy shall ring,
    The Lord Omnipotent is King.

2. The Lord is King! who, then, shall dare
    Resist His will, distrust His care,
Or murmur at His wise decrees,
    Or doubt His royal promises?

3. The Lord is King! child of the dust,
    The Judge of all the earth is just;
Holy and true are all His ways:
    Let every creature speak His praise.

4. He reigns! ye saints, exalt your strains;
    Your God is King, your Father reigns;
And He is at the Father's side,
    The Man of love, the Crucified.

5. Come, make your wants, your burdens, known;
    He will present them at the Throne;
And angel-bands are waiting there,
    His messages of love to bear.

7

6. Alike pervaded by His eye,
All parts of His dominion lie,
This world of ours, and worlds unseen;
And thin the boundary between.

One Lord, one empire, all secures;
He reigns, and life and death are yours:
Through earth and heaven one song shall ring,
The Lord Omnipotent is King.

10   11 S.

*" Let them praise the name of the Lord;
for he commanded, and they were
created."*

1. PRAISE the Lord of heaven, praise Him in the
      height,
   Praise Him, all ye angels; praise Him, stars and
      light;
   Praise Him, skies, and waters, which above the
      skies,
   When His word commanded, 'stablished did
      arise.

2. Praise the Lord, ye fountains of the deeps and
      seas,
   Rocks and hills and mountains, cedars and all
      trees;
   Praise Him, clouds and vapours, snow and hail
      and fire,
   Stormy wind, fulfilling only His desire.

3. Praise Him, fowls and cattle, princes and all
      kings,
   Praise Him, men and maidens, all created things;
   For the name of God is excellent alone;
   Over earth His footstool, over heaven His throne.

11 8, 7.

" Praise ye the Lord from the heavens :
praise him in the heights."

1. PRAISE the Lord! ye heavens, adore Him;
Praise Him, angels, in the height;
Sun and moon, rejoice before Him,
Praise Him, all ye stars of light.

2. Praise the Lord! for He hath spoken;
Worlds His mighty voice obeyed;
Laws that never shall be broken,
For their guidance He hath made.

3. Praise the Lord! for He is glorious;
Never shall His promise fail;
God hath made His saints victorious,
Sin and death shall not prevail.

4. Praise the God of our salvation;
Hosts on high, His power proclaim;
Heaven and earth, and all creation,
Laud and magnify His name!

12 11, 10.

" Praise ye the Lord : O give thanks
unto the Lord, for he is good."

1. PRAISE ye Jehovah, praise the Lord most holy,
Who cheers the contrite, girds with strength
the weak;
Praise Him who will with glory crown the lowly,
And with salvation beautify the meek.

2. Praise ye the Lord, for all His loving-kindness,
And all the tender mercy He hath shown;
Praise Him who pardons all our sin and blind-
ness,
And calls us sons, and takes us for His own.

9

3. Praise ye Jehovah, source of every blessing,
    Before His gifts earth's richest boons are dim;
  Resting in Him, His peace and joy possessing,
    All things are ours, for we have all in Him.

4. Praise ye the Father, God the Lord who gave us,
    With full and perfect love, His only Son;
  Praise ye the Son who died Himself to save us;
    Praise ye the Spirit, praise the Three in One.

13   IO, II.

" His name alone is excellent; his glory
is above the earth and heaven."

1. O WORSHIP the King all-glorious above,
  O gratefully sing His power and His love —
  Our shield and defender, the Ancient of Days,
  Pavilioned in splendour, and girded with praise.

2. O tell of His might, O sing of His grace,
  Whose robe is the light, whose canopy, space!
  His chariots of wrath deep thunder-clouds form,
  And dark is His path on the wings of the storm.

3. The earth with its store of wonders untold,
  Almighty! Thy power hath founded of old;
  Hath stablished it fast by a changeless decree,
  And round it hath cast, like a mantle, the sea.

4. Thy bountiful care what tongue can recite?
  It breathes in the air, it shines in the light,
  It streams from the hills, it descends to the plain,
  And sweetly distils in the dew and the rain.

5. Frail children of dust, and feeble as frail,
  In Thee do we trust, nor find Thee to fail;
  Thy mercies how tender! how firm to the end!
  Our Maker, Defender, Redeemer, and Friend!

essing,
s are dim;
ssessing,
n Him.

o gave us,
Son;
save us;
e in One.

IO, II.

: his glory
ven."

ve —
Days,
a praise.

e,
space!
ds form,
e storm.

ld,
ld;
ecree,
sea.

e?
t,
plain,
n.

;
end!
end!

6. O measureless Might! ineffable Love!
   While angels delight to hymn Thee above,
   The humbler creation, though feeble their lays,
   With true adoration shall lisp to Thy praise.

14   **8s.**

"Who can utter the mighty acts of the
Lord? who can show forth all his
praise?"

1. O God! of good the unfathomed sea!
   Who would not give his heart to Thee?
      Who would not love Thee with his might?
   O Jesus, lover of mankind,
   Who would not his whole soul and mind,
      With all his strength, to Thee unite?

2. Thou shin'st with everlasting rays;
   Before the insufferable blaze,
      Angels with both wings veil their eyes;
   Yet free as air Thy bounty streams
   On all Thy works; Thy mercy's beams
      Diffusive as Thy sun's arise.

3. High throned on heaven's eternal hill,
   In number, weight, and measure still,
      Thou sweetly orderest all that is;
   And yet Thou deign'st to come to me,
   And guide my steps, that I with Thee
      Enthroned, may reign in endless bliss.

4. Fountain of good! all blessing flows
   From Thee; no want Thy fulness knows:
      What but Thyself canst Thou desire?
   Yet, self-sufficient as Thou art,
   Thou dost desire my worthless heart;
      This, only this, dost Thou require.

15

8, 6.

*"If we walk in the light as he is in the
light, we have fellowship one with
another, and the blood of Jesus Christ
his Son cleanseth us from all sin."*

1. ETERNAL Light! eternal Light!
   How pure the soul must be,
When, placed within Thy searching sight,
It shrinks not, but with calm delight
   Can live, and look on Thee!

2. The spirits that surround Thy throne
   May bear the burning bliss;
But that is surely theirs alone,
Since they have never, never known
   A fallen world like this.

3. Oh! how shall I, whose native sphere
   Is dark, whose mind is dim,
Before the Ineffable appear,
And on my naked spirit bear
   That uncreated beam?

4. There is a way for man to rise
   To that sublime abode;
An offering and a sacrifice,
A Holy Spirit's energies,
   An Advocate with God.

5. These, these prepare us for the sight
   Of holiness above:
The sons of ignorance and night
May dwell in the Eternal Light,
   Through the Eternal Love.

8, 6.

he is in the
hip one with
Jesus Christ
m all sin."

g sight,
ht

ne

n

re

---

16   C. M.

" The high and lofty One that inhabiteth
eternity."

1. My God, how wonderful Thou art,
   Thy majesty how bright!
How beautiful Thy mercy-seat,
   In depths of burning light!

2. How dread are Thine eternal years,
   O everlasting Lord!
By prostrate spirits day and night
   Incessantly adored!

3. How wonderful, how beautiful,
   The sight of Thee must be, —
Thine endless wisdom, boundless power,
   And awful purity!

4. Oh, how I fear Thee, living God,
   With deepest, tenderest fears!
And worship Thee with trembling hope,
   And penitential tears.

5. Yet I may love Thee too, O Lord,
   Almighty as Thou art;
For thou hast stooped to ask of me
   The love of my poor heart.

---

17   **6, 8, 3.**

" The Lord is in his holy temple: let all
the earth keep silence before him."

1. GOD reveals His presence:
Let us now adore Him,
And with awe appear before Him:
   God is in His temple,

All within keep silence,
Prostrate lie with deepest reverence.
    Him alone
    God we own, —
Him our God and Saviour:
Praise His name for ever.

2.   God reveals His presence:
Hear the harps resounding!
See the crowds the throne surrounding!
   "Holy, holy, holy,"
Hear the hymn ascending,
Angels, saints, their voices blending!
    Bow Thine ear
    To us here:
Hearken, O Lord Jesus,
To our meaner praises.

3.   O Thou Fount of blessing,
Purify my spirit,
Trusting only in Thy merit:
   Like the holy angels,
Who behold Thy glory,
May I ceaselessly adore Thee.
    Let Thy will,
    Ever still,
Rule Thy church terrestrial,
As the hosts celestial.

4.   Jesus, dwell within me;
Whilst on earth I tarry,
Make me Thy blest sanctuary:
   Then on angel pinions,
Waft me to those regions
Filled with bright seraphic legions.
    May this hope
    Bear me up,
Till these eyes for ever
Gaze on Thee, my Saviour.

18 8, 7, 4.

"Let every thing that hath breath praise the Lord."

1. PRAISE, my soul, the King of heaven;
   To His feet thy tribute bring;
   Ransomed, healed, restored, forgiven,
   Who like thee His praise should sing?
   Praise Him, praise Him,
   Praise the everlasting King!

2. Praise Him for His grace and favour
   To our fathers in distress;
   Praise Him, still the same for ever,
   Slow to chide, and swift to bless.
   Praise Him, praise Him,
   Glorious in His faithfulness.

3. Father-like He tends and spares us;
   Well our feeble frame He knows;
   In His hands He gently bears us,
   Rescues us from all our foes.
   Praise Him, praise Him,
   Widely as His mercy flows.

4. Angels in the height, adore Him;
   Ye behold Him face to face:
   Sun and moon, bow down before Him;
   Dwellers all in time and space.
   Praise Him, praise Him,
   Praise with us the God of grace.

19 8, 7.

"Thine is the kingdom, O Lord, and thou art exalted as head above all."

1. SING praise to God who reigns above,
   The God of all creation,
   The God of power, the God of love,
   The God of our salvation;

15

With healing balm my soul He fills,
And every faithless murmur stills:
    To God all praise and glory!

2. The Angel-host, O King of kings,
        Thy praise for ever telling,
    In earth and sky all living things
        Beneath Thy shadow dwelling,
    Adore the wisdom which could span,
    And power which formed creation's plan ·
        To God all praise and glory!

3. What God's almighty power hath made,
        His gracious mercy keepeth;
    By morning glow or evening shade
        His watchful eye ne'er sleepeth;
    Within the kingdom of His might,
    Lo! all is just, and all is right:
        To God all praise and glory!

4. O ye who bear Christ's holy name,
        Give God all praise and glory!
    All ye who own His power, proclaim
        Aloud the wondrous story;
    Cast each false idol from His throne:
    The Lord is God, and He alone:
        To God all praise and glory!

20   10, 4.

"My help cometh from the Lord."

1. UNTO the hills around do I lift up
        My longing eyes:
    O whence for me shall my salvation come,
        From whence arise?
    From God the Lord doth come my certain aid,
    From God the Lord, who heaven and earth hath
        made.

2. He will not suffer that thy foot be moved:
    Safe shalt thou be.
No careless slumber shall His eyelids close,
    Who keepeth thee.
Behold, He sleepeth not, He slumbereth ne'er,
Who keepeth Israel in His holy care.

3. Jehovah is Himself thy Keeper true —
    Thy changeless shade,
Jehovah evermore on thy right hand
    Himself hath made.
And thee no sun by day shall ever smite,
No moon shall harm thee in the silent night.

4. From every evil shall He keep thy soul,
    From every sin:
Jehovah shall preserve thy going out,
    Thy coming in.
Above thee watching, He whom we adore
Shall keep thee henceforth, yea, for evermore.

21   7s.

*" The morning stars sang together, and
all the sons of God shouted for joy."*

1. SONGS of praise the angels sang,
    Heaven with hallelujahs rang,
    When Jehovah's work begun,
    When He spake, and it was done.

2. Songs of praise awoke the morn,
    When the Prince of Peace was born:
    Songs of praise arose, when He
    Captive led captivity.

3. Heaven and earth must pass away;
    Songs of praise shall crown that day;
    God will make new heavens and earth;
    Songs of praise shall hail their birth.

4. And shall man alone be dumb
Till that glorious kingdom come?
No: the Church delights to raise
Psalms, and hymns, and songs of praise.

5. Saints below, with heart and voice,
Still in songs of praise rejoice;
Learning here, by faith and love,
Songs of praise to sing above.

6. Borne upon their latest breath,
Songs of praise shall conquer death;
Then, amidst eternal joy,
Songs of praise their powers employ.

22
7s.

"His mercy endureth for ever."

1. LET us with a gladsome mind
Praise the Lord, for He is kind;
For His mercies shall endure,
Ever faithful, ever sure.

2. Let us sound His name abroad,
For of gods He is the God;
For His mercies shall endure,
Ever faithful, ever sure.

3. He, with all-commanding might,
Filled the new-made world with light;
For His mercies shall endure,
Ever faithful, ever sure.

4. All things living He doth feed;
His full hand supplies their need;
For His mercies shall endure,
Ever faithful, ever sure.

5. He His chosen race did bless
In the wasteful wilderness;
For His mercies shall endure,
Ever faithful, ever sure.

6. He hath with a piteous eye
Looked upon our misery;
For His mercies shall endure,
Ever faithful, ever sure.

7. Let us, then, with gladsome mind,
Praise the Lord, for He is kind;
For His mercies shall endure,
Ever faithful, ever sure.

23   6, 8, 4.

*" This is my name for ever, and this is
my memorial unto all generations."*

1. THE God of Abraham praise,
Who reigns enthroned above,
Ancient of everlasting days,
And God of love!
Jehovah! Great I AM!
By earth and heaven confest,
I bow, and bless the sacred Name,
For ever blest.

2. The God of Abraham praise,
At whose supreme command
From earth I rise, and seek the joys
At His right hand.
I all on earth forsake,
Its wisdom, fame, and power;
And Him my only portion make,
My shield and tower.

3. He by Himself hath sworn;
  I on His oath depend;
I shall, on eagle's wings upborne,
    To heaven ascend:
  I shall behold His face,
  I shall His power adore,
And sing the wonders of His grace,
    For evermore.

4. The goodly land I see,
  With peace and plenty blest,
A land of sacred liberty
    And endless rest;
  There milk and honey flow,
  And oil and wine abound,
And trees of life for ever grow,
    With mercy crowned.

5. There dwells the Lord our King,
  The Lord our Righteousness,
Triumphant o'er the world and sin:
    The Prince of Peace,
  On Zion's sacred height,
  His kingdom still maintains,
And, glorious with His saints in light,
    For ever reigns.

6. The whole triumphant host
  Give thanks to God on high:
"Hail! Father, Son, and Holy Ghost!"
    They ever cry.
  Hail! Abraham's God and mine!
  I join the heavenly lays;
All might and majesty are Thine,
    And endless praise.

24

C. M.

" Thy way is in the sea, and thy path
in the great waters, and thy footsteps
are not known."

1. GOD moves in a mysterious way,
   His wonders to perform;
He plants His footsteps in the sea,
   And rides upon the storm.

2. Deep in unfathomable mines
   Of never-failing skill,
He treasures up His bright designs,
   And works His sovereign will.

3. Ye fearful saints, fresh courage take;
   The clouds ye so much dread
Are big with mercy, and shall break
   In blessings on your head.

4. Judge not the Lord by feeble sense,
   But trust Him for His grace;
Behind a frowning providence
   He hides a smiling face.

5. His purposes will ripen fast,
   Unfolding every hour;
The bud may have a bitter taste,
   But sweet will be the flower.

6. Blind unbelief is sure to err,
   And scan His work in vain;
God is His own interpreter,
   And He will make it plain.

25   C. M.

" They cry unto the Lord in their trouble."

1. How are Thy servants blest, O Lord !
   How sure is their defence !
   Eternal Wisdom is their guide,
   Their help, Omnipotence.

2. In foreign realms, and lands remote,
   Supported by Thy care,
   Through burning climes they pass unhurt,
   And breathe in tainted air.

3. When by the dreadful tempest borne
   High on the broken wave,
   They know Thou art not slow to hear,
   Nor impotent to save.

4. The storm is laid, the winds retire,
   Obedient to Thy will ;
   The sea, that roars at Thy command,
   At thy command is still.

5. In midst of dangers, fears, and deaths,
   Thy goodness we adore ;
   We praise Thee for Thy mercies past,
   And humbly hope for more.

6. Our life, whilst Thou preservest life,
   A sacrifice shall be ;
   And death, when death shall be our lot,
   Shall join our souls to Thee.

26   L. M.

" Thou hast holden me by my right hand."

1. GREAT God, we sing that mighty hand
   By which supported still we stand :
   The opening year Thy mercy shows,
   That mercy crowns it till it close.

2. By day, by night, at home, abroad,
   Still are we guarded by our God;
   By His incessant bounty fed,
   By His unerring counsel led.

3. With grateful hearts the past we own;
   The future, all to us unknown,
   We to Thy guardian care commit,
   And peaceful leave before Thy feet.

4. In scenes exalted or depressed,
   Thou art our joy, and Thou our rest;
   Thy goodness all our hopes shall raise,
   Adored through all our changing days.

5. When death shall interrupt these songs,
   And seal in silence mortal tongues,
   Our Helper, God, in whom we trust,
   Shall keep our souls, and guard our dust.

27   7, 6.

*" Thou art the same, and thy years shall
have no end."*

1. O GOD, the Rock of Ages,
      Who evermore hast been,
   What time the tempest rages,
      Our dwelling-place serene:
   Before Thy first créations,
      O Lord, the same as now,
   To endless generations
      The Everlasting Thou!

2. Our years are like the shadows
      On sunny hills that lie;
   Or grasses in the meadows,
      That blossom but to die:

23

A sleep, a dream, a story
By strangers quickly told ;
An unremaining glory
Of things that soon are old.

3. O Thou who canst not slumber,
Whose light grows never pale,
Teach us aright to number
Our years before they fail.
On us Thy mercy lighten,
On us Thy goodness rest,
And let Thy Spirit brighten
The hearts Thyself hast blessed.

4. Lord, crown our faith's endeavour
With beauty and with grace,
Till, clothed in light for ever,
We see Thee face to face :
A joy no language measures,
A fountain brimming o'er,
An endless flow of pleasures,
An ocean without shore.

28   L. M.

" The heavens declare the glory of God."

1. THE spacious firmament on high,
With all the blue ethereal sky,
And spangled heavens, a shining frame,
Their great Original proclaim.

2. The unwearied sun, from day to day,
Does his Creator's power display,
And publishes to every land
The work of an Almighty hand.

3. Soon as the evening shades prevail,
The moon takes up the wondrous tale,

And nightly to the listening earth
Repeats the story of her birth;

4. While all the stars that round her burn,
And all the planets in their turn,
Confirm the tidings as they roll,
And spread the truth from pole to pole.

5. What though in solemn silence all
Move round the dark terrestrial ball?
What though no real voice, nor sound,
Amidst their radiant orbs be found?

6. In reason's ear they all rejoice,
And utter forth a glorious voice;
Forever singing, as they shine,
" The Hand that made us is divine."

29   7s.

" His kingdom ruleth over all."

1. SOVEREIGN Ruler of the skies,
Ever gracious, ever wise,
All my times are in Thy hand;
All events at Thy command.

2. He that formed me in the womb,
He shall guide me to the tomb:
All my times shall ever be
Ordered by His wise decree.

3. Times of sickness, times of health,
Times of penury and wealth,
Times of trial and of grief,
Times of triumph and relief,

4. Times the tempter's power to prove,
Times to taste a Saviour's love:

All must come, and last, and end,
As shall please my heavenly Friend.

5. Plagues and deaths around me fly;
Till He bids, I cannot die;
Not a single shaft can hit
Till the God of love sees fit.

6. O Thou gracious, wise, and just!
In Thy hands my life I trust:
Have I something dearer still?
I resign it to Thy will.

7. Thee at all times will I bless;
Having Thee, I all possess:
How can I bereavèd be,
Since I cannot part with Thee?

30

C. M.

*"Lord, thou hast been our dwelling-place
in all generations."*

1. O GOD, our help in ages past,
Our hope for years to come,
Our shelter from the stormy blast,
And our eternal home:

2. Under the shadow of Thy throne
Thy saints have dwelt secure;
Sufficient is Thine arm alone,
And our defence is sure.

3. Before the hills in order stood,
Or earth received her frame,
From everlasting Thou art God,
To endless years the same.

4. A thousand ages in Thy sight
   Are like an evening gone;
Short as the watch that ends the night
   Before the rising sun.

5. The busy tribes of flesh and blood,
   With all their lives and cares,
Are carried downward by the flood,
   And lost in following years.

6. Time, like an ever-rolling stream,
   Bears all its sons away;
They fly forgotten, as a dream
   Dies at the opening day.

7. O God, our help in ages past,
   Our hope for years to come,
Be Thou our guard while troubles last,
   And our eternal home.

. M.

-place

31   6, 7.

" My tongue also shall talk of thy right-
eousness all the day long."

1. Now thank we all our God,
   With heart, and hands, and voices,
Who wondrous things hath done,
   In whom His world rejoices;
Who, from our mother's arms,
   Hath blessed us on our way
With countless gifts of love,
   And still is ours to-day.

2. Oh, may this bounteous God
   Through all our life be near us,
With ever joyful hearts
   And blessèd peace to cheer us,

And keep us in His grace,
And guide us when perplexed,
And free us from all ills
In this world and the next!

3. All prais; and thanks to God
The Father now be given,
The Son, and Him who reigns
With them in highest heaven:
The one eternal God
Whom earth and heaven adore,
For thus it was, is now,
And shall be evermore.

32   S. M.

" Cast thy burden upon the Lord, and
he shall sustain thee."

1. How gentle God's commands,
How kind His precepts are!
Come, cast your burdens on the Lord,
And trust His constant care.

2. While Providence supports,
Let saints securely dwell;
That Hand, which bears all nature up,
Shall guide His children well.

3. Why should this anxious load
Press down your weary mind?
Haste to your heavenly Father's throne,
And sweet refreshment find.

4. His goodness stands approved
Down to the present day:
I'll drop my burden at His feet,
And bear a song away.

33 C. M.

*" How great is thy goodness which thou
hast laid up for them that fear thee."*

1. WHEN all Thy mercies, O my God!
    My rising soul surveys,
Transported with the view, I'm lost
    In wonder, love, and praise.

2. O how shall words, with equal warmth,
    The gratitude declare
That glows within my ravished heart!
    But Thou canst read it there.

3. Thy Providence my life sustained,
    And all my wants redrest,
When in the silent womb I lay,
    And hung upon the breast.

4. To all my weak complaints and cries
    Thy mercy lent an ear,
Ere yet my feeble thoughts had learn'd
    To form themselves in prayer.

5. Unnumbered comforts to my soul
    Thy tender care bestowed,
Before my infant heart conceived
    From whom these comforts flowed.

6. When in the slippery paths of youth,
    With heedless steps I ran,
Thine arm, unseen, conveyed me safe,
    And led me up to man:

7. Through hidden dangers, toils, and deaths,
    It gently cleared my way;
And through the pleasing snares of vice,
    More to be feared than they.

8. When worn with sickness, oft hast Thou
   With health renewed my face;
   And, when in sins and sorrows sunk,
   Revived my soul with grace.

9. Thy bounteous hand with worldly bliss
   Hath made my cup run o'er;
   And, in a kind and faithful friend,
   Hath doubled all my store.

10. Ten thousand thousand precious gifts
    My daily thanks employ;
    Nor is the least a cheerful heart,
    That tastes these gifts with joy.

11. Through every per'od of my life
    Thy goodness I'll proclaim;
    And after death, in distant worlds,
    Resume the glorious theme.

12. When nature fails, and day and night
    Divide Thy works no more,
    My ever-grateful heart, O Lord,
    Thy mercy shall adore.

13. Through all eternity to Thee
    A joyful song I'll raise;
    For, oh! eternity's too short
    To utter all Thy praise.

34   8, 4.

"Freely ye have received, freely give."

1. O LORD of heaven, and earth, and sea,
   To Thee all praise and glory be;
   How shall we shew our love to Thee,
       Who givest all?

2. The golden sunshine, vernal air,
   Sweet flowers and fruit, Thy love declare;
   When harvests ripen, Thou art there,
       Who givest all.

3. For peaceful homes, and healthful days,
   For all the blessings earth displays,
   We owe Thee thankfulness and praise,
       Who givest all.

4. Thou didst not spare Thine only Son,
   But gav'st Him for a world undone,
   And freely with that Blessed One
       Thou givest all.

5. Thou giv'st the Holy Spirit's dower,
   Spirit of life, and love, and power,
   And dost His sevenfold graces shower
       Upon us all.

6. For souls redeemed, for sins forgiven,
   For means of grace and hopes of heaven,
   Father, what can to Thee be given,
       Who givest all?

7. We lose what on ourselves we spend,
   We have as treasure without end
   Whatever, Lord, to Thee we lend,
       Who givest all.

8. Whatever, Lord, we lend to Thee,
   Repaid a thousand-fold will be;
   Then gladly will we give to Thee,
       Who givest all;

9. To Thee, from whom we all derive
   Our life, our gifts, our power to give:
   O may we ever with Thee live,
       Who givest all.

II. — *JESUS CHRIST.*

*" Glory to God in the highest, and on earth
peace, good will toward men."*

1. HARK! the herald angels sing
Glory to the new-born King,
Peace on earth, and mercy mild,
God and sinners reconciled.
Joyful, all ye nations, rise,
Join the triumph of the skies;
With the angelic host proclaim,
Christ is born in Bethlehem.
    Hark! the herald angels sing
    Glory to the new-born King.

2. Christ, by highest heaven adored,
Christ, the Everlasting Lord,
Late in time behold Him come,
Offspring of a Virgin's womb.
Veiled in flesh the Godhead see!
Hail the Incarnate Deity!
Pleased as Man with men to dwell,
Jesus, our Emmanuel.
    Hark! the herald angels sing
    Glory to the new-born King!

3. Hail, the heaven-born Prince of Peace!
   Hail, the Sun of Righteousness!
   Light and life to all He brings,
   Risen with healing in His wings.
   Mild, He lays His glory by,
   Born that man no more may die,
   Born to raise the sons of earth,
   Born to give them second birth.
    Hark! the herald angels sing
    Glory to the new-born King.

36   7s.

" When they saw the star, they rejoiced."

1. As with gladness men of old
   Did the guiding star behold;
   As with joy they hailed its light,
   Leading onward, beaming bright;
   So, most gracious Lord, may we
   Evermore be led by Thee.

2. As with joyful steps they sped
   To that lowly manger-bed,
   There to bend the knee before
   Him whom heaven and earth adore;
   So may we with willing feet
   Ever seek Thy mercy-seat.

3. As they offered gifts most rare
   At that cradle rude and bare,
   So may we with holy joy,
   Pure and free from sin's alloy,
   All our costliest treasures bring,
   Christ, to Thee, our heavenly King.

4. Holy Jesus, every day
   Keep us in the narrow way;

And, when earthly things are past,
Bring our ransomed souls, at last,
Where they need no star to guide,
Where no clouds Thy glory hide.

5. In the heavenly country bright
Need they no created light;
Thou its Light, its Joy, its Crown,
Thou its Sun which goes not down;
There for ever may we sing
Hallelujahs to our King,

37   8, 7.

" There was with the angel a multitude
of the heavenly host praising God."

1. HARK! what mean those holy voices,
Sweetly sounding through the skies?
Lo! the angelic host rejoices;
Heavenly hallelujahs rise.
Listen to the wondrous story
Which they chant in hymns of joy;
" Glory in the highest, glory!
Glory be to God on high!

2. " Peace on earth, good-will from heaven,
Reaching far as man is found;
Souls redeemed, and men forgiven:
Loud our golden harps shall sound.
Christ is born, the great Anointed;
Heaven and earth, His praises sing!
Oh, receive whom God appointed
For your Prophet, Priest, and King.

3. " Hasten, mortals, to adore Him,
Learn His name, and taste His joy
Till in heaven ye sing before Him,
'Glory be to God most high!'"

Let us learn the wondrous story
   Of our great Redeemer's birth;
Spread the brightness of His glory,
   Till it cover all the earth.

38   P. M.

" Let us now go even unto Bethlehem."

1.   O COME, all ye faithful,
       Joyfully triumphant,
To Bethlehem hasten now with glad accord:
       Lo! in a manger
       Lies the King of angels;
O come, let us adore Him, Christ the Lord!

2.   Though true God of true God,
       Light of light eternal,
Our lowly nature He hath not abhorred:
       Son of the Father,
       Not made, but begotten:
O come, let us adore Him, Christ the Lord!

3.   Raise, raise, choirs of angels!
       Songs of loudest triumph,
Through heaven's high arches be your praises
       Now to our God be   [poured:
       Glory in the highest;
O come, let us adore Him, Christ the Lord!

4.   Amen! Lord, we bless Thee,
       Born for our salvation,
O Jesus! for ever be Thy name adored:
       Word of the Father,
       Now in flesh appearing:
O come, let us adore Him, Christ the Lord!

39   8, 7.

"The Word was made flesh."

1. O BLESSED night! O rich delight!
   When, joy with wonder blending,
   To us from heaven a Son was given,
   Angelic hosts attending.

2. For when, in thrall from Adam's fall
   The world in death was lying,
   In flesh like mine, the Life divine
   Rose sun-like o'er the dying.

3. O God of Might! Eternal Light!
   In swaddling-bands they bound Thee;
   Thrust from the hall to lowly stall,
   The herd was gathered round Thee.

4. That cradled Child lay mute and mild,
   That Word whose voice is thunder;
   The world's great Light withdrew from sight;
   Oh, who can solve the wonder!

5. God stoops to dwell in lowly cell,
   Nor shame nor want refusing;
   He leaves His throne, His foes to own,
   For heaven a manger choosing.

40   C. M.

"I bring you good tidings of great joy."

1. JOY to the world! the Lord is come!
   Let earth receive her King;
   Let every heart prepare Him room,
   And heaven and nature sing.

2. Joy to the earth! the Saviour reigns!
    Let men their songs employ,
While fields and floods, rocks, hills, and plains,
    Repeat the sounding joy.

3. No more let sins and sorrows grow,
    Nor thorns infest the ground;
He comes to make His blessings flow
    Far as the curse is found.

4. He rules the world with truth and grace,
    And makes the nations prove
The glories of His righteousness,
    And wonders of His love.

41   L. M.

*"Himself took our infirmities, and bare
our sicknesses."*

1. AT even, ere the sun was set,
    The sick, O Lord, around Thee lay;
Oh, in what divers pains they met!
    Oh, with what joy they went away!

2. Once more 'tis eventide, and we,
    Oppressed with various ills, draw near;
What if Thy form we cannot see?
    We know and feel that Thou art here.

3. O Saviour Christ, our woes dispel;
    For some are sick, and some are sad,
And some have never loved Thee well,
    And some have left the love they had.

4. And some have found the world is vain,
    Yet from the world they break not free;
And some have friends who give them pain,
    Yet have not sought a friend in Thee;

5. And none, O Lord, have perfect rest,
   For none are wholly free from sin;
   And they who fain would serve Thee best
   Are conscious most of wrong within.

6. O Saviour Christ, Thou too art Man;
   Thou hast been troubled, tempted, tried;
   Thy kind but searching glance can scan
   The very wounds that shame would hide.

7. Thy touch has still its ancient power;
   No word from Thee can fruitless fall;
   Hear in this solemn evening hour,
   And in Thy mercy heal us all.

42   7s.

" Lord, if thou wilt, thou canst make me clean."

1. On the shore of Galilee
   Walked a leper silently;
   Heard the eager people cry:
   "Lo, the Healer passeth by!"

2. Came the man of solitude,
   Shunned by all the multitude,
   And with all his heart's accord
   Worshipped low before the Lord.

3. "If Thou wilt!" the leper cried;
   "Be thou clean!" the Lord replied.
   Faith enough to come and crave;
   Power enough to stand and save.

4. Jesus quick put forth His hand,
   Token of a sweet command,
   Overjoyed the leper's soul,
   For the Lord hath touched him whole.

5. Oh, thou Healer, still the same!
  Speak to me Thy mighty name,
  While for joy I worship Thee,
  Like the man of Galilee.

6. Touch me, Lord, destroy my sin;
  Touch me, Jesus, make me clean;
  Sinner I, but Saviour Thou!
  Touch, O Christ, my sullied brow!

43

8s.

" Jesus of Nazareth passeth by."

1. WHAT means this eager, anxious throng,
  Which moves with busy haste along, —
  These wondrous gatherings day by day?
  What means this strange commotion, pray?
  In accents hushed the throng reply ·
  " Jesus of Nazareth passeth by."

2. Who is this Jesus? Why should he
  The city move so mightily?
  A passing stranger, has he skill
  To move the multitude at will?
  Again the stirring notes reply:
  " Jesus of Nazareth passeth by."

3. Jesus! 'tis He who once below
  Man's pathway trod, 'mid pain and woe;
  And burdened ones, where'er He came,
  Brought out their sick, and deaf, and lame;
  The blind rejoiced to hear the cry:
  "Jesus of Nazareth passeth by."

4. Again He comes! From place to place
  His holy footprints we can trace.

He pauseth at our threshold, — nay,
He enters, — condescends to stay.
Shall we not gladly raise the cry:
"Jesus of Nazareth passeth by?"

5. Ho! all ye heavy laden, come:
Here's pardon, comfort, rest, and home.
Ye wanderers from a Father's face,
Return, accept His proffered grace.
Ye tempted ones, there's refuge nigh:
"Jesus of Nazareth passeth by."

6. But if you still this call refuse,
And all His wondrous love abuse,
Soon will He sadly from you turn,
Your bitter prayer for pardon spurn.
"Too late! too late!" will be the cry:
"Jesus of Nazareth has passed by."

44

C. M.

"Jesus . . . a prophet mighty in deed."

1. THINE arm, O Lord, in days of old,
Was strong to heal and save;
It triumphed o'er disease and death,
O'er darkness and the grave;
To Thee they went, — the blind, the dumb,
The palsied and the lame,
The leper with his tainted life,
The sick with fevered frame.

2. And, lo! Thy touch brought life and health,
Gave speech and strength and sight;
And youth renewed and frenzy calmed
Owned Thee the Lord of light.

And now, O Lord, be near to bless,
　Almighty as of yore,
In crowded street, by restless couch,
　As by Gennesaret's shore.

3. Be Thou our great Deliverer still,
　　Thou Lord of life and death;
Restore and quicken, soothe and bless,
　With Thine Almighty breath;
To hands that work, and eyes that see,
　Give wisdom's heavenly lore,
That whole and sick, and weak and strong,
　May praise Thee evermore.

45　　　　　　　　　　　C. M.

" I am the way, and the truth, and the life."

1. THOU art the Way: to Thee alone
　　From sin and death we flee;
And he who would the Father seek,
　Must seek Him, Lord, by Thee.

2. Thou art the Truth: Thy word alone
　　True wisdom can impart:
Thou only canst inform the mind,
　And purify the heart.

3. Thou art the Life: the rending tomb
　　Proclaims Thy conquering arm;
And those who put their trust in Thee,
　Nor death nor hell shall harm.

4. Thou art the Way, the Truth, the Life:
　　Grant us that Way to know,
That Truth to keep, that Life to win,
　Whose joys eternal flow.

46 L. M.

*" Behold, thy King cometh unto thee . . .
lowly, and riding upon an ass, and
upon a colt the foal of an ass."*

1. RIDE on, ride on in majesty!
   Hark! all the tribes Hosanna cry:
   O Saviour meek, pursue Thy road,
   With palms and scattered garments strewed.

2. Ride on, ride on in majesty!
   In lowly pomp ride on to die:
   O Christ, Thy triumphs now begin
   O'er captive death and conquered sin.

3. Ride on, ride on in majesty!
   The wingèd squadrons of the sky
   Look down with sad and wondering eyes
   To see the approaching sacrifice.

4. Ride on, ride on in majesty!
   The last and fiercest strife is nigh:
   The Father on His sapphire throne
   Awaits His own anointed Son.

5. Ride on, ride on in majesty!
   In lowly pomp ride on to die:
   Bow Thy meek head to mortal pain,
   Then take, O God, Thy power, and reign.

47 8, 6.

*" The Lord hath laid on him the iniquity
of us all."*

1. O CHRIST, what burdens bowed Thy head!
   Our load was laid on Thee;
   Thou stoodest in the sinner's stead,
   Bearing all ill for me.

42

A victim led, Thy blood was shed;
   Now there's no load for me.

2. The Father lifted up His rod —
   .O Christ, it fell on Thee!
Thou wast sore stricken of Thy God,
   There's not one stroke for me.
Thy tears, Thy blood, beneath it flowed;
   Thy bruising healeth me.

3. The Holy One did hide His face —
   O Christ, 'twas hid from Thee!
Dumb darkness wrapt Thy soul a space, —
   The darkness due to me.
But now that face of radiant grace
   Shines forth in light on me.

4. For me, Lord Jesus, Thou hast died,
   And I have died in Thee!
Thou'rt risen; my bonds are all untied;
   And now Thou liv'st in me.
When purified, made white and tried,
   Thy glory then for me.

48   L. M.

*" God forbid that I should glory, save in
the cross of our Lord Jesus Christ."*

1. WE sing the praise of Him who died, —
   Of Him who died upon the cross:
The sinner's hope let men deride,
   For this we count the world but loss.

2. Inscribed upon the cross we see,
   In shining letters, " God is love;"
He bears our sins upon the tree,
   He brings us mercy from above.

3. The cross — it takes our guilt away;
    It holds the fainting spirit up;
It cheers with hope the gloomy day,
    And sweetens every bitter cup.

4. It makes the coward spirit brave,
    And nerves the feeble arm for fight;
It takes its terror from the grave,
    And gilds the bed of death with light.

5. The balm of life, the cure of woe,
    The measure and the pledge of love,
The sinner's refuge here below,
    The angels' theme in heaven above.

49   L. M.

*" What things were gain to me, those I
counted loss for Christ."*

1. WHEN I survey the wondrous cross
    On which the Prince of glory died,
My richest gain I count but loss,
    And pour contempt on all my pride.

2. Forbid it, Lord, that I should boast,
    Save in the death of Christ my God;
All the vain things that charm me most
    I sacrifice them to His blood.

3. See from His head, His hands, His feet,
    Sorrow and love flow mingled down!
 · Did e'er such love and sorrow meet,
    Or thorns compose so rich a crown?

4. Were the whole realm of nature mine,
    That were a present far too small;
Love so amazing, so divine,
    Demands my soul, my life, my all.

50   **7, 6.**

"Surely he hath borne our griefs."

1. O LAMB of God, once wounded,
      With grief and pain weighed down,
   Thy sacred head surrounded
      With thorns, Thine only crown!

2. How pale art Thou with anguish,
      With sore abuse and scorn!
   How does that visage languish,
      Which once was bright as morn!

3. O Lord of life and glory,
      What bliss till now was Thine!
   I read the wondrous story,
      I joy to call Thee mine.

4. Thy grief and Thy compassion
      Were all for sinners' gain;
   Mine, mine was the transgression,
      But Thine the deadly pain.

5. What language shall I borrow,
      To praise Thee, Heavenly Friend,
   For this Thy dying sorrow,
      Thy pity without end?

6. Lord, make me Thine for ever,
      Nor let me faithless prove;
   Oh, let me never, never
      Abuse such dying love!

7. Be near me, Lord, when dying;
      Show Thou Thyself to me;
   And, for my succour flying,
      Come, Lord, to set me free:

45

8. These eyes, new faith receiving,
   From Jesus shall not move:
For he who dies believing,
   Dies safely through Thy love.

51   L. M.

" He hath covered me with the robe of righteousness."

1. JESUS, Thy blood and righteousness
   My beauty are, my glorious dress;
   'Midst flaming worlds, in these arrayed,
   With joy shall I lift up my head.

2. Bold shall I stand in Thy great day;
   For who aught to my charge shall lay?
   Fully absolved through these I am,
   From sin and fear, from guilt and shame.

3. When from the dust of death I rise,
   To claim my mansion in the skies,
   Even then, this shall be all my plea,
   Jesus hath lived, hath died for me.

4. Jesus, be endless praise to Thee,
   Whose boundless mercy hath for me —
   For me, a full atonement made,
   An everlasting ransom paid.

5. O let the dead now hear Thy voice;
   Now bid Thy banished ones rejoice;
   Their beauty this, their glorious dress,
   Jesus, Thy blood and righteousness.

52　　　　　　　　　8, 7, 4.

" It is finished."

1. HARK! the voice of love and mercy
　　Sounds aloud from Calvary,
　See, the rocks are rent asunder,
　　Darkness veils the mid-day sky;
　　　" It is finished!"
　Hear the dying Saviour cry.

2. " It is finished!" Oh, what pleasure
　　Do these precious words afford!
　Heavenly blessings without measure
　　Flow to us from Christ the Lord.
　　　" It is finished!"
　Saints, the dying words record.

3. Finished all the types and shadows
　　Of the ceremonial law;
　Finished all that God had promised;
　　Death and hell no more shall awe.
　　　" It is finished!"
　Saints, from hence your comfort draw.

4. Tune your harps anew, ye seraphs,
　　Join to sing the pleasing theme,
　All on earth and all in heaven,
　　Join to praise Immanuel's name.
　　　Hallelujah!
　Glory to the bleeding Lamb!

53　　　　　　　　　6, 8.

" Having therefore boldness to enter into
the holiest by the blood of Jesus."

1. DONE is the work that saves!
　　Once and for ever done!
　Finished the righteousness
　　That clothes the unrighteous one!

The love that blesses us below
Is flowing freely to us now.

2. The sacrifice is o'er;
    The veil is rent in twain;
Sprinkled the mercy-seat
    With blood of victim slain;
Why stand we then without in fear?
The blood divine invites us near.

3. The gate is open wide,
    The new and living way
Is clear and free and bright,
    With love and peace and day;
Into the holiest now we come,
Our present and our endless home.

4. Then to the Lamb once slain
    Be glory, praise, and power,
Who died and lives again,
    Who liveth evermore;
Who loved and washed us in His blood,
Who made us kings and priests to God!

54   7s.

" The fellowship of his sufferings."

1. Go to dark Gethsemane,
    Ye that feel the tempter's power;
Your Redeemer's conflict see;
    Watch with Him one bitter hour;
Turn not from His griefs away;
Learn of Jesus Christ to pray.

2. Follow to the judgment-hall;
    View the Lord of life arraigned.
Oh, the wormwood and the gall!
    Oh, the pangs His soul sustained!

Shun not suffering, shame, or loss;
Learn of Him to bear the cross.

3. Calvary's mournful mountain climb;
   There, adoring at His feet,
Mark that miracle of time —
   God's own sacrifice complete.
"It is finished!" hear Him cry;
Learn of Jesus Christ to die.

4. Early hasten to the tomb,
   Where they laid His breathless clay,
All is solitude and gloom —
   Who hath taken Him away?
Chist is risen; He seeks the skies:
Saviour, teach us so to rise.

55   6, 10.

*" He humbled himself, and became
obedient unto death."*

1. THOU, who didst stoop below
   To drain the cup of woe,
And wear the form of frail mortality,
   Thy blessèd labours done,
   Thy crown of victory won,
Hast passed from earth, passed to Thy home on
   high.

2. It was no path of flowers
   Through this dark world of ours,
Beloved of the Father, Thou didst tread:
   And shall we in dismay
   Shrink from the narrow way,
When clouds and darkness are around it spread?

3. O Thou who art our life,
   Be with us through the strife!

49

Thy own meek head by rudest storms was bowed ;
 Raise Thou our eyes above,
 To see a Father's love
Beam, like a bow of promise, through the cloud.

4. E'en through the awful gloom
 Which hovers o'er the tomb,
That light of love our guiding star shall be ;
 Our spirits shall not dread
 The shadowy way to tread,
Friend, Guardian, Saviour! which doth lead to
 Thee.

56   C. M.

*" Upon the first day of the week, very
early in the morning, they came
unto the sepulchre."*

1. BLEST morning! whose first dawning rays
 Beheld the Son of God
Arise triumphant from the grave,
 And leave His dark abode.

2. Wrapt in the silence of the tomb
 The great Redeemer lay,
Till the revolving skies had brought
 The third, th' appointed day.

3. Hell and the grave combined their force
 To hold our Lord in vain ;
Sudden the Conqueror arose,
 And burst their feeble chain.

4. To Thy great name, Almighty Lord!
 We sacred honours pay,
And loud hosannas shall proclaim
 The triumphs of the day.

5. Salvation and immortal praise
   To our victorious King!
Let heaven and earth, and rocks and seas,
   With glad hosannas ring.

6. To Father, Son, and Holy Ghost,
   The God whom we adore,
Be glory, as it was, and is,
   And shall be evermore.

57   7s.

" He is not here, but is risen."

1. " CHRIST the Lord is risen to-day,"
   Sons of men, and angels, say:
   Raise your joys and triumphs high;
   Sing, ye heavens ; and, earth, reply.

2. Love's redeeming work is done,
   Fought the fight, the battle won:
   Lo! our Sun's eclipse is o'er,
   Lo! He sets in blood no more.

3. Vain the stone, the watch, the seal;
   Christ hath burst the gates of hell;
   Death in vain forbids His rise ;
   Christ hath opened Paradise.

4. Lives again our glorious King ;
   Where, O death, is now thy sting?
   Once He died our souls to save ·
   Where thy victory, O grave ?

5. Soar we now where Christ hath led,
   Following our exalted Head ;
   Made like Him, like Him we rise;
   Ours the cross, the grave, the skies.

51

6. Hail! the Lord of earth and heaven!
   Praise to Thee by both be given;
   Thee we greet triumphant now,
   Hail! the Resurrection Thou!

58   7s.

" Now is Christ risen from the dead."

1. CHRIST the Lord is risen again;
   Christ hath broken every chain;
   Hark! the angels shout for joy,
   Singing evermore on high,
   > Hallelujah!

2. He who gave for us His life,
   Who for us endured the strife,
   Is our Paschal Lamb to-day;
   We too sing for joy, and say,
   > Hallelujah!

3. He who bore all pain and loss,
   Comfortless upon the cross,
   Lives in glory now on high,
   Pleads for us, and hears our cry:
   > Hallelujah!

4. Now He bids us tell abroad
   How the lost may be restored,
   How the penitent forgiven,
   How we too may enter heaven.
   > Hallelujah!

5. Thou, our Paschal Lamb indeed,
   Christ, Thy ransomed people feed;
   Take our sins and guilt away,
   That we all may sing for aye,
   > Hallelujah!

59 S. M.

"The Lord is risen indeed."

1. "THE Lord is risen indeed;"
   Now is His work performed;
Now is the mighty captive freed,
   And Death's strong castle stormed.

2. "The Lord is risen indeed;"
   The Grave has lost his prey;
With Him is risen the ransomed seed,
   To reign in endless day.

3. "The Lord is risen indeed;"
   He lives, to die no more;
He lives, the sinner's cause to plead,
   Whose curse and shame He bore.

4. "The Lord is risen indeed;"
   Attending angels, hear!
Up to the courts of heaven, with speed,
   The joyful tidings bear.

5. Then tune your golden lyres,
   And strike each cheerful chord;
Join, all ye bright celestial choirs,
   To sing our risen Lord!

60 7, 8.

"Because I live, ye shall live also."

1. JESUS lives! no longer now
   Can thy terrors, Death, appal me;
Jesus lives! by this I know,
   Thou, O grave! canst not enthrall me.
Brighter scenes at death commence;
This shall be my confidence.
               Hallelujah

2. Jesus lives! to Him the throne
　　High o'er heaven and earth is given;
I may go where He is gone,
　　Live and reign with Him in heaven.
God through Christ forgives offence;
This shall be my confidence.
　　　　　　　　　　Hallelujah!

3. Jesus lives! who now despairs,
　　Spurns the word which God hath spoken;
Grace to all that word declares,
　　Grace whereby sin's yoke is broken.
Christ rejects not penitence;
This shall be my confidence.
　　　　　　　　　　Hallelujah!

4. Jesus lives! for me He died:
　　Hence will I, to Jesus living,
Pure in heart and act abide,
　　Praise to Him and glory giving.
Freely God doth aid dispense;
This shall be my confidenee.
　　　　　　　　　　Hallelujah!

5. Jesus lives! my heart knows well,
　　Nought from me His love shall sever;
Life, nor death, nor powers of hell,
　　Part me now from Christ for ever.
God will be a sure defence;
This shall be my confidence.
　　　　　　　　　　Hallelujah!

61　　　　　　　　　　　　　　L. M.

"Behold, I am alive for evermore."

1. "I KNOW that my Redeemer lives:"
　　What comfort this assurance gives!
He lives, He lives, who once was dead;
　　He lives, my ever-living Head.

2. He lives, triumphant from the grave,
   He lives eternally to save,
He lives all glorious in the sky,
   He lives exalted there on high.

3. He lives to bless me with His love,
   He lives to plead for me above,
He lives my hungry soul to feed,
   He lives to help in time of need.

4. He lives; and while He lives, I'll sing,
   He lives, my Prophet, Priest, and King,
He lives, my kind, my faithful Friend,
   He lives, and loves me to the end.

5. He lives; all glory to his name!
   He lives, my Jesus, still the same;
O the sweet joy the assurance gives,
   "I know that my Redeemer lives!"

62   S. M.

" Thou hast ascended on high."

1. THOU art gone up on high,
   To mansions in the skies,
And round Thy throne unceasingly
   The songs of praise arise.

2. But we are lingering here
   With sin and care oppressed;
Lord, send Thy promised Comforter,
   And lead us to Thy rest.

3. Thou art gone up on high;
   But Thou didst first come down,
Through earth's most bitter agony
   To pass unto Thy crown.

4. And girt with griefs and fears
    Our onward course must be;
   But only let that path of tears
    Lead us at last to Thee.

5. Thou art gone up on high;
    But Thou shalt come again,
   With all the bright ones of the sky
    Attendant in Thy train.

6. O by Thy saving power,
    So make us live and die,
   That we may stand, in that dread hour,
    At Thy right hand on high!

63   C. M.

" He is Lord of lords, and King of kings."

1. ALL hail the power of Jesus' name!
    Let angels prostrate fall;
   Bring forth the royal diadem,
    To crown Him Lord of all.

2. Crown Him, ye martyrs of your God,
    Who from His altar call;
   Extol the stem of Jesse's rod,
    And crown Him Lord of all.

3. Ye seed of Israel's chosen race,
    Ye ransomed from the fall,
   Hail Him who saves you by His grace,
    And crown Him Lord of all.

4. Ye Gentile sinners! ne'er forget
    The wormword and the gall,
   Go, spread your trophies at His feet,
    And crown him Lord of all.

5. Let every kindred, every tribe,
   On this terrestrial ball,
To Him all majesty ascribe,
   And crown Him Lord of all.

6. Oh that with yonder sacred throng
   We at His feet may fall,
Join in the everlasting song,
   And crown Him Lord of all.

64   S. M.

" On his head were many crowns."

1. CROWN Him with many crowns,
   The Lamb upon His Throne:
Hark how the heavenly anthem drowns
   All music but its own.

2. Awake, my soul, and sing
   Of Him who died for thee,
And hail Him as thy matchless King
   Through all eternity.

3. Crown Him, the Lord of Love;
   Behold His hands and side,
Rich wounds, yet visible above
   In beauty glorified.

4. All hail! Redeemer, hail!
   For Thou hast died for me;
Thy praise shall never, never fail
   Throughout eternity.

65 C. M.

" We see Jesus . . . crowned with glory and honour."

1. THE Head that once was crowned with thorns
    Is crowned with glory now;
   A royal diadem adorns
    The mighty Victor's brow.

2. The highest place that heaven affords
    Is His, is His by right,
   The King of kings and Lord of lords,
    And heaven's eternal light.

3. The joy of all who dwell above,
    The joy of all below,
   To whom He manifests His love,
    And grants His name to know.

4. To them the cross, with all its shame,
    With all its grace, is given;
   Their name an everlasting name,
    Their joy the joy of heaven.

5. They suffer with their Lord below,
    They reign with Him above:
   Their profit and their joy to know
    The mystery of His love.

6. The cross He bore is life and health,
    Though shame and death to Him;
   His people's hope, His people's wealth,
    Their everlasting theme.

66

.M.

with

ns

8, 7.

" I that speak in righteousness, mighty to save."

1. WHO is this that comes from Edom,
    All His raiment stained with blood,
  To the slave proclaiming freedom,
    Bringing and bestowing good,
  Glorious in the garb He wears,
  Glorious in the spoils He bears?

2. 'Tis the Saviour, now victorious,
    Travelling onward in His might;
  'Tis the Saviour, O how glorious
    To His people is the sight!
  Jesus now is strong to save,
  Mighty to redeem the slave.

3. Why that blood His raiment staining?
    'Tis the blood of many slain:
  Of His foes there's none remaining,
    None the contest to maintain;
  Fallen they are, no more to rise,
  All their glory prostrate lies.

4. This the Saviour has effected
    By His mighty arm alone;
  See the throne for Him erected,
    'Tis an everlasting throne!
  'Tis the great reward He gains,
  Glorious fruit of all His pains.

5. Mighty Victor, reign for ever!
    Wear the crown so dearly won;
  Never shall Thy people, never
    Cease to sing what Thou hast done.
  Thou hast fought Thy people's foes;
  Thou wilt heal Thy people's woes.

67

8, 7, 4.

"That at the name of Jesus every knee should bow."

1. LOOK, ye saints! the sight is glorious;
   See the Man of Sorrows now!
From the fight returned victorious,
   Every knee to Him shall bow:
      Crown Him! crown Him!
Crowns become the Victor's brow.

2. Crown the Saviour! angels, crown Him!
   Rich the trophies Jesus brings;
In the seat of power enthrone Him,
   While the vault of heaven rings:
      Crown Him! crown Him!
Crown the Saviour, King of kings!

3. Sinners in derision crowned Him,
   Mocking thus Messiah's claim,—
Saints and angels throng around Him,
   Own His title, praise His name:
      Crown Him! crown Him!
Spread abroad the Victor's fame.

4. Hark, those bursts of acclamation!
   Hark, those loud triumphant chords!
Jesus takes the highest station:
   O what joy the sight affords!
      Crown him! crown Him!
King of kings, and Lord of lords.

68

IOS.

" Thou art worthy, O Lord, to receive glory and honour and power."

1. BLESSING and honour and glory and power,
   Wisdom and riches and strength evermore,

Give ye to Him who our battle hath won,
Whose are the kingdom, the crown, and the
   throne.

2. Past are the darkness, the storm, and the war,
Come is the radiance that sparkled afar,
Breaketh the gleam of the day without end,
Riseth the sun that shall never descend.

3. Ever ascendeth the song and the joy,
Ever descendeth the love from on high,
Blessing and honour and glory and praise,
This is the theme of the hymns that we raise.

4. Life of all life, and true light of all light,
Star of the dawning, unchangingly bright,
Sun of the Salem whose light is the Lamb,
Theme of the ever-new, ever-glad psalm!

5. Give we the glory and praise to the Lamb,
Take we the robe and the harp and the palm,
Sing we the song of the Lamb that was slain,
Dying in weakness, but rising to reign.

69   8, 7.

" A name which is above every name."

1. PRINCE of Peace and Lord of Glory,
     Humbly at Thy throne we bow;
   Saints and angels all adore Thee,
     We would join their worship now.
   Jesus, who wast scorned, forsaken,
     Smitten, wounded, crucified,
   We, with love and trust unshaken,
     Take Thee as our Hope and Guide.

2. Watchful Shepherd, mighty Saviour,
   Tender Healer, ever near!
 King of kings, by whose free favour
   We o'ercome each foe and fear!—
 Be our Leader in all duty;
   Be our Surety to the end;
 Be our Diadem of Beauty,
   Our Belovèd and our Friend!

3. Son of Man, despised, rejected,
   Holy, harmless, undefiled;
 By Thy life we are protected,
   By Thy death we're reconciled:
 Rock of Ages, sure Foundation,
   King of Saints and Judge of all;
 Only source of our salvation, —
   On Thy Blessed Name we call!

4. Prophet, Priest, and King victorious;
   High-Priest, Altar, Sacrifice,
 Light of light, and Sun most glorious,
   Draw to Thee our sin-dimmed eyes!
 We are pilgrims lone and strangers,
   And we need Thy constant care
 Till we pass earth's toils and dangers
   And Thy final triumph share.

70   6, 5.

" Every day will I bless thee."

1. SAVIOUR, blessed Saviour,
   Listen whilst we sing,
 Hearts and voices raising
   Praises to our King;
 All we have to offer,
   All we hope to be,
 Body, soul, and spirit,
   All we yield to Thee.

2. Nearer, ever nearer,
      Christ, we draw to Thee;
   Deep in adoration
      Bending low the knee;
   Thou for our redemption
      Cam'st on earth to die;
   Thou, that we might follow,
      Hast gone up on high.

3. Great and ever greater
      Are Thy mercies here,
   True and everlasting
      Are the glories there,
   Where no pain, or sorrow,
      Toil, or care, is known,
   Where the angel-legions
      Circle round Thy throne.

4. Clearer still and clearer
      Dawns the light from heaven,
   In our sadness bringing
      News of sin forgiven;
   Life has lost its shadows,
      Pure the light within;
   Thou hast shed Thy radiance
      On a world of sin.

5. Onward, ever onward,
      Journeying o'er the road
   Worn by saints before us,
      Journeying on to God
   Leaving all behind us,
      May we hasten on,
   Backward never looking
      Till the prize is won.

6. Bliss, all bliss excelling,
      When the ransomed soul,
   Earthly toils forgetting,
      Finds its promised goal;

Where, in joys unheard of,
  Saints with angels sing,
Never weary raising
  Praises to their King.

71   **8, 7.**

" A friend of publicans and sinners."

1. ONE there is, above all others,
  Well deserves the name of Friend;
His is love beyond a brother's,
  Costly, free, and knows no end:
They who once His kindness prove,
Find it everlasting love.

2. Which of all our friends, to save us,
  Could or would have shed their blood?
But our Jesus died to have us
  Reconciled in Him to God:
This was boundless love indeed;
Jesus is a Friend in need.

3. When He lived on earth abasèd,
  Friend of sinners was His name;
Now above all glory raisèd,
  He rejoices in the same:
Still He calls them brethren, friends,
And to all their wants attends.

4. Could we bear from one another
  What He daily bears from us?
Yet this glorious Friend and Brother
  Loves us though we treat Him thus:
Though for good we render ill,
He accounts us brethren still.

5. O for grace our hearts to soften !
   Teach us, Lord, at length to love :
We, alas ! forget too often
   What a Friend we have above ;
But when home our souls are brought,
We will love Thee as we ought.

72　　　　　　　　　　　　　8s.

*"I speak of the things which I have
made touching the King."*

1. My heart is full of Christ, and longs
   Its glorious matter to declare !
Of Him I make my loftier songs,
   I cannot from His praise forbear ;
My ready tongue makes haste to sing
The glories of my heavenly King.

2. Fairer than all the heaven-born race,
   Perfect in comeliness Thou art ;
Replenished are Thy lips with grace,
   And full of love Thy tender heart :
God ever blest ! we bow the knee,
And own all fulness dwells in Thee.

3. Gird on Thy thigh the Spirit's sword,
   And take to Thee Thy power divine ;
Stir up Thy strength, almighty Lord,
   All power and majesty are Thine :
Assert Thy worship and renown ;
   O all-redeeming God, come down

4. Come and maintain Thy righteous cause,
   And let Thy glorious toil succeed :
Dispread the victory of Thy cross,
   Ride on and prosper in Thy deed ;
Through earth triumphantly ride on,
And reign in every heart alone.

73   6, 8.

"His name shall be called Wonderful."

1. JOIN all the glorious names
    Of wisdom, love, and power,
That ever mortals knew,
    That angels ever bore;
All are too mean to speak His worth,
Too mean to set my Saviour forth.

2. Great Prophet of my God,
    My tongue would bless Thy name;
By Thee the joyful news
    Of our salvation came;
The joyful news of sins forgiven,
Of hell subdued, and peace with Heaven.

3. Jesus, my great High Priest,
    Offered His blood and died;
My guilty conscience seeks
    No sacrifice beside:
His powerful blood did once atone,
And now it pleads before the throne.

4. O Thou Almighty Lord,
    My Conqueror and my King,
Thy sceptre and Thy sword,
    Thy reigning grace, I sing:
Thine is the power: behold, I sit
In willing bonds before Thy feet.

74   L. M.

*"He that cometh to me shall never hunger,
and he that believeth on me shall never
thirst."*

1. JESUS, Thou joy of loving hearts,
    Thou fount of life, Thou light of men!
From the best bliss that earth imparts
    We turn unfilled to Thee again.

2. Thy truth unchanged hath ever stood;
    Thou savest those that on Thee call:
  To them that seek Thee, Thou art good,
    To them that find Thee, all in all!

3. We taste Thee, O Thou living bread,
    And long to feast upon Thee still;
  We drink of Thee, the fountain-head,
    And thirst our souls from Thee to fill.

4. Our restless spirits yearn for Thee,
    Where'er our changeful lot is cast;
  Glad when Thy gracious smile we see,
    Blest when our faith can hold Thee fast.

5. O Jesus, ever with us stay!
    Make all our moments calm and bright;
  Chase the dark night of sin away;
    Shed o'er the world Thy holy light.

75   C. M.

*" The love of Christ which passeth know-
ledge."*

1. JESUS, the very thought of Thee
    With sweetness fills my breast:
  But sweeter far Thy face to see,
    And in Thy presence rest.

2. Nor voice can sing, nor heart can frame,
    Nor can the memory find
  A sweeter sound than Thy blest name,
    O Saviour of mankind!

3. O Hope of every contrite heart,
    O Joy of all the meek,
  To those who fall how kind Thou art,
    How good to those who seek!

4. But what to those who find ? Ah ! this
 Nor tongue nor pen can show ;
The love of Jesus, what it is
 None but His loved ones know.

5. Jesus, our only joy be Thou,
 As Thou our prize wilt be ;
Jesus, be Thou our glory now,
 And through eternity.

76   **7s.**

" Thou shalt call his name Jesus."

1. JESUS ! name of wondrous love,
 Name all other names above !
 Unto which must every knee
 Bow in deep humility.

2. Jesus ! name of priceless worth
 To the fallen sons of earth,
 For the promise that it gave —
 " Jesus shall His people save."

3. Jesus ! name of mercy mild,
 Given to the Holy Child,
 When the cup of human woe
 First He tasted here below.

4. Jesus ! only name that's given
 Under all the mighty heaven,
 Whereby man, to sin enslaved,
 Bursts his fetters, and is saved.

5. Jesus ! name of wondrous love,
 Human name of God above !
 Pleading only this, we flee,
 Helpless, O our God, to Thee.

77
C. M.

" Thy name is as ointment poured forth."

1. How sweet the Name of Jesus sounds
    In a believer's ear!
It soothes his sorrows, heals his wounds,
    And drives away his fear.

2. It makes the wounded spirit whole,
    And calms the troubled breast;
'Tis manna to the hungry soul,
    And to the weary rest.

3. Dear Name! the rock on which I build,
    My shield and hiding-place;
My never-failing treasury, filled
    With boundless stores of grace.

4. Jesus, my Shepherd, Husband, Friend,
    My Prophet, Priest, and King,
My Lord, my Life, my Way, my End,
    Accept the praise I bring.

5. Weak is the effort of my heart,
    And cold my warmest thought,
But when I see Thee as Thou art,
    I'll praise Thee as I ought.

6. Till then I would Thy love proclaim
    With every fleeting breath:
And may the music of Thy name
    Refresh my soul in death!

78
C. M.

" My soul doth magnify the Lord."

1. O FOR a thousand tongues to sing
    My great Redeemer's praise,
The glories of my God and King,
    The triumphs of His grace!

2. My gracious Master, and my God,
   Assist me to proclaim,
   To spread through all the earth abroad
   The honours of Thy name.

3. Jesus ! the name that charms our fears,
   That bids our sorrows cease ;
   'Tis music in the sinner's ears,
   'Tis life, and health, and peace.

4. He breaks the power of cancelled sin,
   He sets the prisoner free ;
   His blood can make the foulest clean,
   His blood avails for me.

5. He speaks, and, listening to His voice,
   New life the dead receive ;
   The mournful, broken hearts rejoice,
   The humble poor believe.

6. Hear Him, ye deaf ; His praise, ye dumb,
   Your loosened tongues employ ;
   Ye blind, behold your Saviour come,
   And leap, ye lame, for joy.

79   8, 11.

*" Blessed is he that cometh in the name
of the Lord : Hosanna in the highest."*

1. HOSANNA to the living Lord !
   Hosanna to the Incarnate Word !
   To Christ, Creator, Saviour, King,
   Let earth, let heaven hosanna sing.
   Hosanna, Lord ! Hosanna in the highest !

2. O Saviour, with protecting care
   Return to this Thy house of prayer ;

Assembled in Thy sacred Name,
Where we Thy parting promise claim.
   Hosanna, Lord! Hosanna in the highest!

3. But chiefest, in our cleansèd breast,
Eternal, bid Thy Spirit rest;
And make our secret soul to be
A temple pure, and worthy Thee.
   Hosanna, Lord! Hosanna in the highest!

4. So, in the last and dreadful day,
When earth and heaven shall melt away,
Thy flock, redeemed from sinful stain,
Shall swell the sound of praise again.
   Hosanna, Lord! Hosanna in the highest!

80   8, 7.

" Wherefore God also hath highly ex-
alted him."

1. HAIL, Thou once despisèd Jesus!
   Hail, Thou Galilean King!
Thou didst suffer to release us;
   Thou didst free salvation bring.
Hail, Thou agonizing Saviour,
   Bearer of our sin and shame;
By Thy merits we find favour;
   Life is given through Thy name.

2. Paschal Lamb, by God appointed,
   All our sins were on Thee laid;
By Almighty love anointed,
   Thou hast full atonement made.
All thy people are forgiven
   Through the virtue of Thy blood,
Opened is the gate of heaven;
   Peace is made 'twixt man and God.

71

3. Jesus, hail! enthroned in glory,
  There for ever to abide;
All the heavenly hosts adore Thee,
  Seated at Thy Father's side.
There for sinners Thou art pleading,
  There Thou dost our place prepare,
Ever for us interceding,
  Till in glory we appear.

4. Worship, honour, power, and blessing
  Thou art worthy to receive;
Loudest praises without ceasing
  Meet it is for us to give.
Help, ye bright angelic spirits,
  Bring your sweetest, noblest lays;
Help to sing our Saviour's merits,
  Help to chant Immanuel's praise!

81

6, 4.

"Worthy is the Lamb that was slain."

1. GLORY to God on high!
  Let earth to heaven reply;
    Praise ye His name:
  His love and grace adore,
  Who all our sorrows bore;
  And praise Him evermore;
    Worthy the Lamb!

2. Jesus, our Lord and God,
  Bore sin's tremendous load;
    Praise ye His name:
  Tell what His arm hath done,
  What spoils from death He won;
  Sing His great name alone;
    Worthy the Lamb!

3. While they around the throne
Join cheerfully in one,
    Praising His name,
We who have felt His blood
Sealing our peace with God,
Sound His high praise abroad;
    Worthy the Lamb!

4. Join, all the ransomed race,
Our Lord and God to bless;
    Praise ye His name:
In Him we will rejoice,
Making a gladsome noise,
Shouting with heart and voice,
    Worthy the Lamb!

82   S. M.

"They sing the song of Moses, the servant of God, and the song of the Lamb."

1. AWAKE, and sing the song
    Of Moses and the Lamb;
Wake every heart and every tongue,
    To praise the Saviour's name.

2. Sing of His dying love,
    Sing of His rising power;
Sing how He intercedes above
    For those whose sins He bore.

3. Sing on your heavenly way,
    Ye ransomed sinners, sing;
Sing on, rejoicing every day
    In Christ the eternal King.

4. Soon shall ye hear Him say,
    Ye blessèd children, come;

Soon will He call you hence away,
And take His wanderers home.

5. There shall each raptured tongue
His endless praise proclaim,
And sing in sweeter notes the song
Of Moses and the Lamb.

83   7s.

" When he ascended up on high, he led captivity captive."

1. GLORY, glory to our King!
Crowns unfading wreathe His head:
Jesus is the name we sing,
Jesus, risen from the dead,
Jesus, Conqueror o'er the grave,
Jesus, mighty now to save.

2. Jesus is gone up on high;
Angels come to meet their King;
Shouts triumphant rend the sky,
While the Victor's praise they sing:
'Open now, ye heavenly gates!
'Tis the King of Glory waits.'

3. Now behold Him high enthroned,
Glory beaming from His face,
By adoring angels owned
God of holiness and grace.
O for hearts and tongues to sing,
'Glory, glory to our King!'

4. Jesus, on Thy people shine;
Warm our hearts and tune our tongues,
That with angels we may join,
Share their bliss and swell their songs:
Glory, honour, praise, and power,
Lord, be Thine for evermore.

74

84   6, 8.

" He must reign, till he hath put all ene-
mies under his feet."

1. REJOICE, the Lord is King;
　　Your Lord and King adore;
　Mortals, give thanks and sing,
　　And triumph evermore:
　Lift up your heart, lift up your voice;
　Rejoice, again I say, rejoice.

2. Jesus the Saviour reigns,
　　The God of truth and love;
　When He had purged our stains,
　　He took His seat above:
　Lift up your heart, lift up your voice;
　Rejoice, again I say, rejoice.

3. His kingdom cannot fail,
　　He rules o'er earth and heaven;
　The keys of death and hell
　　Are to our Jesus given:
　Lift up your heart, lift up your voice;
　Rejoice, again I say, rejoice.

4. He sits at God's right hand,
　　Till all His foes submit,
　And bow to His command,
　　And fall beneath His feet:
　Lift up your heart, lift up your voice;
　Rejoice, again I say, rejoice.

5. Rejoice in glorious hope;
　　Jesus, the Judge, shall come,
　And take His servants up
　　To their eternal home:
　We soon shall hear th' archangel's voice,
　The trump of God shall sound, rejoice.

85   8, 7.

" Waiting for the consolation of Israel."

1. COME, Thou long-expected Jesus,
   Born to set Thy people free;
   From our fears and sins release us,
   Let us find our rest in Thee.

2. Israel's strength and consolation,
   Hope of all the earth Thou art;
   Dear Desire of every nation,
   Joy of every longing heart.

3. Born Thy people to deliver;
   Born a child and yet a king;
   Born to reign in us for ever;
   Now Thy gracious kingdom bring.

4. By Thine own eternal Spirit
   Rule in all our hearts alone;
   By Thine all-sufficient merit
   Raise us to Thy glorious throne.

86   L. M.

*" Behold, the Lord cometh with ten thou-
sands of his saints."*

1. THE Lord will come, the earth shall quake,
   The hills their fixèd seat forsake;
   And, withering, from the vault of night
   The stars withdraw their feeble light.

2. The Lord will come; but not the same
   As once in lowly form He came;
   A silent Lamb to slaughter led,
   The bruised, the suffering, and the dead.

3. The Lord will come, a dreadful form,
   With wreath of flame, and robe of storm,
   On cherub wings, and wings of wind,
   Anointed Judge of humankind.

4. Can this be He who wont to stray
   A pilgrim on the world's highway,
   By power oppressed, and mocked by pride,
   The Nazarene, the Crucified?

5. Go, tyrants! to the rocks complain,
   Go, seek the mountain's cleft in vain;
   But faith, victorious o'er the tomb,
   Shall sing for joy, the Lord is come!

87   8, 7, 4.

"Behold, he cometh with clouds."

1. Lo! He comes, with clouds descending,
   Once for favoured sinners slain;
   Thousand thousand saints attending
   Swell the triumph of His train;
   Hallelujah!
   God appears on earth to reign.

2. Every eye shall now behold Him
   Robed in dreadful majesty;
   Those who set at naught and sold Him,
   Pierced and nailed Him to the tree,
   Deeply wailing,
   Shall the true Messiah see.

3. Every island, sea, and mountain,
   Heaven and earth, shall flee away;
   All who hate Him must, confounded,
   Hear the trump proclaim the day;
   Come to judgment,
   Come to judgment, come away!

4. Now redemption, long expected,
    See in solemn pomp appear !
 All His saints, by man rejected,
    Now shall meet Him in the air:
       Hallelujah !
 See the day of God appear !

5. Yea, amen, let all adore Thee,
    High on Thine eternal throne !
 Saviour, take the power and glory ;
    Claim the kingdom for Thine own :
       O come quickly !
 Everlasting God, come down.

88   8, 7, 4.

" The coming of the Lord draweth nigh."

1. CHRIST is coming ! let creation
    From her groans and travail cease ;
 Let the glorious proclamation
    Hope restore, and faith increase :
       Christ is coming !
 Come, Thou blessed Prince of Peace.

2. Earth can now but tell the story
    Of Thy bitter cross and pain ;
 She shall yet behold Thy glory,
    When Thou comest back to reign :
       Christ is coming !
 Let each heart repeat the strain.

3. Long Thine exiles have been pining,
    Far from rest, and home, and Thee ;
 But in heavenly vestures shining,
    Soon they shall Thy glory see :
       Christ is coming !
 Haste the joyous jubilee.

4. With that blessed hope before us,
    Let no harp remain unstrung;
  Let the mighty advent-chorus
    Onward roll from tongue to tongue :
      Christ is coming !
      Come, Lord Jesus, quickly come '

89   P. M.

> *" At midnight there was a cry made,*
> *Behold, the bridegroom cometh ;*
> *go ye out to meet him."*

1. WAKE, awake, for night is flying,
  The watchmen on the heights are crying;
    Awake, Jerusalem, at last !
  Midnight hears the welcome voices,
  And at the thrilling cry rejoices,
    Come forth, ye virgins, night is past
      The Bridegroom comes, awake,
      Your lamps with gladness take ;
        Hallelujah !
  And for His marriage feast prepare,
  For you must go to meet Him there.

2. Zion hears the watchmen singing,
  And all her heart with joy is springing,
    She wakes, she rises from her gloom ;
  For her Lord comes down all-glorious,
  The strong in grace, in truth victorious,
    Her Star is risen, her Light is come !
      Ah, come, Thou blessed One,
      God's own beloved Son ;
        Hallelujah !
  We follow till the halls we see
  Where Thou hast bid us sup with Thee.

3. Now let all the heavens adore Thee,
  And men and angels sing before Thee
    With harp and cymbal's clearest tone ;

Of one pearl each shining portal,
Where we are with the choir immortal
  Of angels round Thy dazzling throne ;
    Nor eye hath seen, nor ear
    Hath yet attained to hear,
      What there is ours ;
But we rejoice, and sing to Thee
Our hymn of joy eternally.

III. — *THE HOLY SPIRIT.*

90 S. M.

" He dwelleth with you, and shall be in you."

1. COME, Holy Spirit, come,
   Let Thy bright beams arise;
   Dispel the darkness from our minds,
   And open all our eyes.

2. Cheer our desponding hearts,
   Thou heavenly Paraclete;
   Give us to lie with humble hop
   At our Redeemer's feet.

3. Revive our drooping fait
   Our doubts and fears remove,
   And kindle in our breasts the flame
   Of never-dying love.

4. Convince us of our sin;
   Then lead to Jesus' blood,
   And to our wondering view reveal
   The secret love of God.

5. 'Tis Thine to cleanse the heart,
   To sanctify the soul,
   To pour fresh life in every part,
   And new create the whole.

6. Dwell, therefore, in our hearts;
   Our minds from bondage free;
   Then we shall know and praise and love
   The Father, Son, and Thee.

91   L. M.

" The love of God is shed abroad in our
hearts, by the Holy Ghost, which is
given unto us."

1. COME, gracious Spirit, heavenly Dove,
   With light and comfort from above :
   Be Thou our Guardian, Thou our Guide,
   O'er every thought and step preside.

2. The light of truth to us display,
   And make us know and love Thy way;
   Plant holy fear in every heart,
   That we from God may ne'er depart.

3. Lead us to holiness, the road
   Which we must take to dwell with God;
   Lead us to Christ, the living way,
   Nor let us from His pastures stray.

4. Lead us to God, our final rest,
   To be with Him for ever blest;
   Lead us to heaven, its bliss to share —
   Fulness of joy for ever there.

92   C. M.

" Thy Spirit is good : lead me into the land
of uprightness."

1. COME, Holy Spirit, heavenly Dove,
   With all Thy quickening powers,
   Kindle a flame of sacred love
   In these cold hearts of ours.

2. In vain we tune our formal songs,
   In vain we strive to rise;
   Hosannas languish on our tongues,
   And our devotion dies.

3. And shall we then for ever live
   At this poor dying rate?
   Our love so faint, so cold to Thee,
   And Thine to us so great!

4. Come, Holy Spirit, heavenly Dove,
   With all Thy quickening powers;
   Come, shed abroad a Saviour's love,
   And that shall kindle ours.

93   7s.

" The earnest of the Spirit in our hearts."

1. GRACIOUS Spirit, Love divine,
   Let Thy light within me shine;
   All my guilty fears remove,
   Fill me full of heaven and love.

2. Speak Thy pardoning grace to me,
   Set the burdened sinner free;
   Lead me to the Lamb of God,
   Wash me in His precious blood.

3. Life and peace to me impart,
   Seal salvation on my heart;
   Breathe Thyself into my breast,
   Earnest of immortal rest. .

4. Let me never from Thee stray,
   Keep me in the narrow way;
   Fill my soul with joy divine,
   Keep me, Lord, for ever Thine.

94   S. M.

*Ye shall be baptized with the Holy
Ghost, not many days hence."*

1. LORD God, the Holy Ghost,
   In this accepted hour,
As on the day of Pentecost,
   Descend in all Thy power:
   We meet with one accord
   In our appointed place,
And wait the promise of our Lord,
   The Spirit of all grace.

2. Like mighty rushing wind
   Upon the waves beneath,
Move with one impulse every mind,
   One soul, one feeling breathe ·
   The young, the old, inspire·
   With wisdom from above,
And give us hearts and tongues of fire
   To pray, and praise, and love.

3. Spirit of light, explore
   And chase our gloom away,
With lustre shining more and more
   Unto the perfect day.
   Spirit of truth, be Thou
   In life and death our guide .
O Spirit of adoption, now
   May we be sanctified !

95   L. M.

*" Ye have an unction from the Holy One,
and ye know all things."*

1. COME, Holy Ghost, our souls inspire,
   And lighten with celestial fire ;
Thou the anointing Spirit art,
Who dost Thy sevenfold gifts impart.

2. Thy blessed unction from above
Is comfort, life, and fire of love;
Enable with perpetual light
The dulness of our blindèd sight.

3. Anoint and cheer our soilèd face
With the abundance of Thy grace:
Keep far our foes, give peace at home;
Where Thou art guide no ill can come.

4. Teach us to know the Father, Son,
And Thee, of Both, to be but One;
That, through the ages all along,
This may be our endless song:
  Praise to Thy eternal merit,
  Father, Son, and Holy Spirit.

96   C. M.

" When he, the Spirit of truth, is come,
he will guide you into all truth."

1. COME, Holy Ghost, our hearts inspire ·
  Let us Thine influence prove,
Source of the old prophetic fire,
  Fountain of light and love.

2. Come, Holy Ghost, for, moved by Thee,
  The prophets wrote and spoke;
Unlock the truth, Thyself the key,
  Unseal the sacred book.

3. Expand Thy wings, celestial Dove,
  Brood o'er our nature's night;
On our disordered spirits move,
  And let there now be light.

4. God through Himself we then shall know,
  If Thou within us shine,
And sound, with all Thy saints below,
  The depths of love divine.

"The Comforter, which is the Holy Ghost."

1. COME, Thou Holy Paraclete,
   And from Thy celestial seat
       Send Thy light and brilliancy.

2. Father of the poor, draw near;
   Giver of all gifts, be here:
       Come, the soul's true radiancy.

3. Come, of Comforters the best,
   Of the soul the sweetest guest,
       Come in toil refreshingly.

4. Thou in labour rest most sweet,
   Thou art shadow from the heat,
       Comfort in adversity.

5. O Thou Light, most pure and blest,
   Shine within the inmost breast
       Of Thy faithful company.

6. Where Thou art not, man hath nought;
   Every holy deed and thought
       Comes from Thy Divinity.

7. What is soilèd, make Thou pure;
   What is wounded, work its cure;
       What is parchèd, fructify;

8. What is rigid, gently bend;
   What is frozen, warmly tend;
       Straighten what goes erringly.

9. Fill Thy faithful, who confide
   In Thy power to guard and guide,
       With Thy sevenfold Mystery.

10. Here Thy grace and virtue send;
     Grant salvation in the end,
     And in heaven felicity.

98   8s.

"The Spirit of God moved upon the face
of the waters."

1. CREATOR Spirit! by whose aid
   The world's foundations first were laid,
   Come, visit every humble mind;
   Come, pour Thy joys on all mankind;
   From sin and sorrow set us free,
   And make us temples worthy Thee.

2. O source of uncreated light,
   The Father's promised Paraclete!
   Thrice holy fount, thrice holy fire,
   Our hearts with heavenly love inspire;
   Come, and Thy sacred unction bring,
   To sanctify us while we sing.

3. Plenteous of grace, descend from high
   Rich in Thy sevenfold energy;
   Give us Thyself, that we may see
   The Father and the Son by Thee;
   Make us eternal truths receive,
   And practise all that we believe.

4. Immortal honour, endless fame,
   Attend the Almighty Father's name:
   The Saviour Son be glorified,
   Who for lost man's redemption died
   And equal adoration be,
   Eternal Paraclete, to Thee.

IMAGE EVALUATION
TEST TARGET (MT-3)

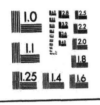

|← 6" →|

Photographic
Sciences
Corporation

23 WEST MAIN STREET
WEBSTER, N.Y. 14580
(716) 872-4503

99 L. M.

"I will pour out my Spirit upon all flesh."

1. O SPIRIT of the living God!
   In all Thy plenitude of grace,
   Where'er the foot of man hath trod,
   Descend on our apostate race!

2. Give tongues of fire and hearts of love,
   To preach the reconciling word;
   Give power and unction from above,
   Whene'er the joyful sound is heard.

3. Be darkness, at Thy coming, light;
   Confusion, order in Thy path;
   Souls without strength inspire with might;
   Bid mercy triumph over wrath.

4. O Spirit of the Lord! prepare
   All the round earth her God to meet:
   Breathe Thou abroad like morning air,
   Till hearts of stone begin to beat.

5. Baptize the nations; far and nigh
   The triumphs of the cross record;
   The name of Jesus glorify,
   Till every kindred call Him Lord.

100 8, 7.

*"The kingdom of God is . . . righteous-
ness, and peace, and joy in the Holy
Ghost."*

1. HOLY GHOST, dispel our sadness,
   Pierce the clouds of sinful night;
   Come, Thou source of sweetest gladness,
   Breathe Thy life, and spread Thy light.

Loving Spirit, God of peace,
Great distributer of grace,
　Rest upon this congregation;
　Hear, O hear our supplication.

2. From that height which knows no measure,
　As a gracious shower, descend;
Bringing down the richest treasure
　Man can wish, or God can send.
O Thou glory, shining down
From the Father and the Son,
　Grant us Thy illumination;
　Rest upon this congregation.

3. Come, Thou best of all donations
　God can give, or we implore;
Having Thy sweet consolations
　We need wish for nothing more.
Come with unction and with power,
On our souls Thy graces shower;
　Author of the new creation,
　Make our hearts Thy habitation.

101

C. M.

*" There are diversities of gifts, but the
same Spirit."*

1. SPIRIT Divine! attend our prayers,
　And make this house Thy home;
Descend with all Thy gracious powers;
　O come, great Spirit, come!

2. Come as the Light: to us reveal
　Our emptiness and woe;
And lead us in those paths of life
　Where all the righteous go.

3. Come as the Fire, and purge our hearts
   Like sacrificial flame;
   Let our whole soul an offering be
   To our Redeemer's name.

4. Come as the Dew, and sweetly bless
   This consecrated hour;
   May barrenness rejoice to own
   Thy fertilising power.

5. Come as the Dove, and spread Thy wings,
   The wings of peaceful love;
   And let the Church on earth become
   Blest as the Church above.

6. Come as the Wind, with rushing sound
   And Pentecostal grace;
   That all of woman born may see
   The glory of Thy face.

7. Spirit Divine! attend our prayers,
   Make a lost world Thy home;
   Descend with all Thy gracious powers;
   O come, great Spirit, come!

102   8, 6, 4.

*" The Comforter . . . whom I will send
unto you."*

1. OUR blest Redeemer, ere He breathed
   His tender last farewell,
   A Guide, a Comforter, bequeathed
   With us to dwell.

2. He came sweet influence to impart,
   A gracious, willing guest,
   While He can find one humble heart
   Wherein to rest.

3. And His that gentle voice we hear,
    Soft as the breath of even,
  That checks each thought, that calms each fear,
    And speaks of heaven.

4. And every virtue we possess,
    And every conquest won,
  And every thought of holiness
    Are His alone.

5. Spirit of purity and grace,
    Our weakness, pitying, see :
  O make our hearts Thy dwelling-place,
    And worthier Thee.

6. O praise the Father ; praise the Son ;
    Blest Spirit, praise to Thee ;
  All praise to God, the Three in One,
    The One in Three.

103   L. M.

*" The Spirit of God moved upon the face
of the waters."*

1. SPIRIT of God, that moved of old
    Upon the waters' darkened face,
  Come, when our faithless hearts are cold,
    And stir them with an inward grace.

2. Thou that art Power and Peace combined,
    All highest Strength, all purest Love,
  The rushing of the mighty Wind,
    The brooding of the gentle Dove :

3. Come, give us still Thy powerful aid,
    And urge us on, and keep us Thine ;
  Nor leave the hearts that once were made
    Fit temples for Thy grace divine :

4. Nor let us quench Thy sevenfold light;
    But still with softest breathings stir
Our wayward souls — and lead us right,
    O Holy Ghost, the Comforter!

104   C. M.

*" We have received the Spirit of adop-
tion, whereby we cry, Abba, Father."*

1. WHY should the children of a King
    Go mourning all their days?
Great Comforter, descend and bring
    Some tokens of Thy grace.
Dost Thou not dwell in all the saints,
    And seal them heirs of heaven?
When wilt Thou banish my complaints,
    And show my sins forgiven?

2. Assure my conscience of her part
    In the Redeemer's blood;
And bear Thy witness with my heart
    That I am born of God.
Thou art the earnest of His love,
    The pledge of joys to come;
And Thy soft wings, celestial Dove,
    Will safe convey me home.

105   C. M.

*" All scripture is given by inspiration
of God."*

1. THE Spirit breathes upon the Word,
    And brings the truth to sight;
Precepts and promises afford
    A sanctifying light.

2. A glory gilds the sacred page,
   Majestic like the sun;
It gives a light to every age,
   It gives, but borrows none.

3. The hand that gave it still supplies
   The gracious light and heat;
His truths upon the nations rise —
   They rise, but never set.

4. Let everlasting thanks be Thine
   For such a bright display
As makes a world of darkness shine
   With beams of heavenly day.

5. My soul rejoices to pursue
   The steps of Him I love,
Till glory breaks upon my view
   In brighter worlds above.

106   7, 6.

" Holding forth the word of life."

1. O WORD of God incarnate,
      O Wisdom from on high,
   O Truth unchanged, unchanging,
      O Light of our dark sky;
   We praise Thee for the radiance
      That from the hallowed page,
   A lantern to our footsteps,
      Shines on from age to age.

2. The Church from her dear Master
      Received the gift divine,
   And still that light she lifteth
      O'er all the earth to shine.

93

It is the golden casket
    Where gems of truth are stored;
It is the heaven-drawn picture
    Of Christ the living Word.

3. It floateth like a banner
    Before God's host unfurled;
It shineth like a beacon
    Above the darkening world;
It is the chart and compass,
    That o'er life's surging sea,
'Mid mists, and rocks, and quicksands,
    Still guide, O Christ, to Thee.

4. O make Thy Church, dear Saviour,
    A lamp of burnished gold,
To bear before the nations
    Thy true light as of old:
O teach Thy wandering pilgrims
    By this their path to trace,
Till, clouds and darkness ended,
    They see Thee face to face.

107   C. M.

*" Thy statutes have been my songs in the
house of my pilgrimage."*

1. FATHER of mercies, in Thy Word
    What endless glory shines!
For ever be Thy name adored
    For these celestial lines.

2. Here springs of consolation rise
    To cheer the fainting mind;
And thirsty souls receive supplies,
    And sweet refreshment find.

3. Here the Redeemer's welcome voice
   Spreads heavenly peace around;
And life, and everlasting joys,
   Attend the blissful sound.

4. O may these heavenly pages be
   My ever dear delight;
And still new beauties may I see,
   And still increasing light.

5. Divine Instructor, gracious Lord!
   Be Thou for ever near;
Teach me to love Thy sacred word,
   And view my Saviour there.

108
C. M.

" All scripture is given by inspiration of God."

1. How precious is the Book Divine,
   By inspiration given!
Bright as a lamp its doctrines shine,
   To guide our souls to heaven.

2. It sweetly cheers our drooping hearts,
   In this dark vale of tears:
Life, light, and joy it still imparts,
   And quells our rising fears.

3. This lamp, through all the tedious night
   Of life, shall guide our way,
Till we behold the clearer light
   Of an eternal day.

109

C. M.

"The seed is the word of God."

1. ALMIGHTY God : thy word is cast
      Like seed into the ground ;
   Now let the dew of heaven descend,
      And righteous fruits abound.

2. Let not the foe of Christ and man
      This holy seed remove ;
   But give it root in every heart
      To bring forth fruits of love.

3. Let not the world's deceitful cares
      The rising plant destroy,
   But may it yield a hundred-fold
      The fruits of peace and joy.

4. Let not Thy word so kindly sent
      To raise us to Thy throne,
   Return to Thee, and sadly tell
      That we reject Thy Son.

5. Oft as the precious seed is sown,
      Thy quickening grace bestow ;
   That all, whose souls the truth receive,
      Its saving power may know.

96

IV. — CHRISTIAN LIFE.

110

7, 6.

" Unto you therefore which believe he is precious."

1. I NEED Thee, precious Jesus,
   For I am full of sin;
My soul is dark and guilty,
   My heart is dead within;
I need the cleansing fountain
   Where I can always flee,
The blood of Christ most precious,
   The sinner's perfect plea.

2. I need Thee, precious Jesus,
   For I am very poor;
A stranger and a pilgrim
   I have no earthly store:
I need the love of Jesus
   To cheer me on my way,
To guide my doubting footsteps,
   To be my strength and stay.

3. I need Thee, precious Jesus,
   And hope to see Thee soon,
Encircled with the rainbow,
   And seated on Thy throne;

Then with Thy blood-bought children,
My joy shall ever be,
To sing Thy praises, Jesus,
To gaze, my Lord, on Thee.

111   **8s.**

" I will heal their backsliding."

1. WEARY of wandering from my God,
    And now made willing to return,
I hear, and bow me to the rod;
    For Him, not without hope, I mourn:
I have an Advocate above,
A Friend before the throne of love.

2. O Jesus, full of pardoning grace,
    More full of grace than I of sin;
Yet once again I seek Thy face,
    Open Thine arms, and take me in,
And freely my backslidings heal,
And love the faithless sinner still.

3. Thou knowest the way to bring me back,
    My fallen spirit to restore;
Oh, for Thy truth and mercy's sake,
    Forgive, and bid me sin no more;
The ruins of my soul repair,
And make my heart a house of prayer.

4. Ah! give me, Lord, the tender heart
    That trembles at the approach of sin;
A godly fear of sin impart,
    Implant, and root it deep within,
That I may dread Thy gracious power,
And never dare offend Thee more.

112
L. M.

" Behold, I stand at the door and knock."

1. BEHOLD, a Stranger at the door!
   He gently knocks, has knocked before;
   Has waited long, is waiting still;
   You treat no other friend so ill.

2. O lovely attitude! He stands
   With melting heart and laden hands;
   O matchless kindness! and He shows
   This matchless kindness to His foes!

3. Admit Him, for the human breast
   Ne'er entertained so kind a guest;
   No mortal tongue their joy can tell,
   With whom He condescends to dwell.

4. Admit Him, ere His anger burn,
   Lest He depart, and ne'er return;
   Admit Him, or the hour's at hand
   When at His door denied you'll stand.

5. Yet know, nor of the terms complain,
   Where Jesus comes, He comes to reign,
   To reign, and with no partial sway;
   Thoughts must be slain that disobey.

6. Sovereign of souls, Thou Prince of Peace,
   O may Thy gentle reign increase:
   Throw wide the door, each willing mind,
   And be His empire all mankind.

113 C. M.

" Learn of me, and ye shall find rest unto your souls."

1. I HEARD the voice of Jesus say,
     "Come unto Me and rest;
   Lay down, thou weary one, lay down
     Thy head upon My breast!"
   I came to Jesus as I was,
     Weary, and worn, and sad;
   I found in Him a resting-place,
     And He has made me glad.

2. I heard the voice of Jesus say,
     "Behold, I freely give
   The living water; thirsty one,
     Stoop down, and drink, and live!"
   I came to Jesus, and I drank
     Of that life-giving stream;
   My thirst was quenched, my soul revived,
     And now I live in Him.

3. I heard the voice of Jesus say,
     "I am this dark world's light;
   Look unto Me, thy morn shall rise,
     And all thy day be bright."
   I looked to Jesus, and I found
     In Him my star, my sun;
   And in that light of life I'll walk
     Till travelling days are done.

114 7s.

" He beheld the city, and wept over it."

1. LORD, in this Thy mercy's day,
   Ere it pass for aye away,
   On our knees we fall and pray.

2. Holy Jesus, grant us tears,
   Fill us with heart-searching fears,
   Ere that awful doom appears.

3. Lord, on us Thy Spirit pour,
   Kneeling lowly at the door,
   Ere it close for evermore.

4. By Thy night of agony,
   By Thy supplicating cry,
   By Thy willingness to die,

5. By Thy tears of bitter woe
   For Jerusalem below,
   Let us not Thy love forego.

6. Grant us 'neath Thy wings a place,
   Lest we lose this day of grace
   Ere we shall behold Thy face.

7. On Thy love we rest alone,
   And that love will then be known
   By the pardoned round the throne.

115

S. M.

"Behold, now is the accepted time."

1. Now is th' accepted time,
     Now is the day of grace;
   Now, sinners, come without delay,
     And seek the Saviour's face.

2. Now is th' accepted time,
     The Saviour calls to-day;
   To-morrow you may be too late;
     'Tis madness to delay.

3. Now is th' accepted time,
   The Gospel bids you come;
And every promise of His word
   Declares there yet is room.

4. Lord, draw reluctant souls
   To seek a Father's love!
Then shall attendant angels bear
   The joyful news above.

116   L. M.

*" There is joy in the presence of the
    angels of God over one sinner
    that repenteth."*

1. WHO can describe the joys that rise
   Through all the courts of Paradise,
   To see a prodigal return,
   To see an heir of glory born!

2. With joy the Father doth approve
   The fruit of His eternal love;
   The Son with joy looks down, and sees
   The purchase of His agonies.

3. The Spirit takes delight to view
   The holy soul He formed anew;
   And saints and angels join to sing
   The growing empire of their King.

117   8, 6, 4.

" Return unto the Lord thy God."

1. RETURN, O wanderer, to thy home,
   Thy Father calls for thee;
No longer now an exile roam
   In guilt and misery:
      Return, return.

2. Return, O wanderer, to thy home,
   'Tis Jesus calls for thee;
The Spirit and the Bride say, "Come,"
   O now for refuge flee:
      Return, return.

3. Return, O wanderer, to thy home,
   'Tis madness to delay;
There are no pardons in the tomb,
   And brief is mercy's day:
      Return, return.

118   8, 7, 4.

*" Him that cometh unto me, I will in no
wise cast out."*

1. COME, ye sinners, poor and wretched,
      Weak and wounded, sick and sore;
   Jesus ready stands to save you,
      Full of pity joined with power.
         He is able;
      He is willing; doubt no more.

2. Come, ye needy, come and welcome,
      God's free bounty glorify;
   True belief and true repentance,
      Every grace that brings you nigh,
         Without money,
      Come to Jesus Christ, and buy.

3. Come, ye weary, heavy laden,
      Lost and ruined by the fall;
   If you tarry till you're better,
      You will never come at all.
         Not the righteous,
      Sinners, Jesus came to call.

4. Let not conscience make you linger,
      Nor of fitness fondly dream;

All the fitness He requireth
Is to feel your need of Him:
This he gives you,
'Tis the Spirit's rising beam.

5. Lo! the incarnate God, ascended,
Pleads the merit of His blood,
Venture on Him, venture wholly,
Let no other trust intrude:
None but Jesus
Can do helpless sinners good.

119   8, 7, 4.

" A bruised reed shall he not break."

1. COME, ye souls by sin afflicted,
Bowed with fruitless sorrow down;
By the broken law convicted,
Through the cross behold the crown!
Look to Jesus!
Mercy flows through Him alone.

2. Take His easy yoke and wear it;
Love will make obedience sweet;
Christ will give you strength to bear it,
While His wisdom guides your feet
Safe to glory,
Where His ransomed captives meet.

3. Blessèd are the eyes that see Him,
Blessèd the ears that hear His voice;
Blessèd are the souls that trust Him,
And in Him alone rejoice:
His commandments
Then become their happy choice.

4. Sweet as home to pilgrims weary,
Light to newly opened eyes,

Flowing springs in deserts dreary,
Is the rest the cross supplies;
All who taste it
Shall to rest immortal rise.

120   11, 10.

" I will not leave you comfortless."

1. COME, ye disconsolate, where'er ye languish;
Come to the mercy-seat, fervently kneel;
Here bring your wounded hearts, here tell your
anguish;
Earth has no sorrow that Heaven cannot heal.

2. Joy of the desolate, light of the straying,
Hope of the penitent, fadeless and pure,
Here speaks the Comforter, tenderly saying,
Earth has no sorrow that Heaven cannot cure.

3. Here see the Bread of Life; see waters flowing
Forth from the throne of God, pure from
above;
Come to the feast of love; come ever knowing
Earth has no sorrow but Heaven can remove.

121   6, 4, 7.

" Without me ye can do nothing."

1. I NEED Thee every hour,
Most gracious Lord;
No tender voice like Thine
Can peace afford.
I need Thee, O I need Thee;
Every hour I need Thee;
O bless me now, my Saviour!
I come to Thee.

2. I need Thee every hour,
    Stay Thou near by;
  Temptations lose their power
    When Thou art nigh.

3. I need Thee every hour,
    In joy or pain;
  Come quickly and abide,
    Or life is vain.

4. I need Thee every hour;
    Teach me Thy will,
  And Thy rich promises
    In me fulfil.

122   S. M.

*" Not by works of righteousness which
we have done."*

1. NOT what these hands have done
    Can save my guilty soul;
  Not what this toiling flesh has borne
    Can make my spirit whole.

2. Not what I feel or do
    Can give me peace with God;
  Not all my prayers, and sighs, and tears,
    Can bear my awful load.

3. Thy work alone, O Christ,
    Can ease this weight of sin;
  Thy blood alone, O Lamb of God,
    Can give me peace within.

4. Thy love to me, O God,
    Not mine, O Lord, to Thee,
  Can rid me of this dark unrest,
    And set my spirit free.

5. I bless the Christ of God;
   I rest on love divine;
And, with unfaltering lip and heart,
   I call this Saviour mine.

6. I praise the God of grace;
   I trust His truth and might;
He calls me His, I call Him mine,
   My God, my Joy, my Light.

123   7s.

" Justified freely by his grace."

1. NOT in any thing we do,
   Thought that's pure, or word that's true,
   Saviour, would we put our trust:
   Frail as vapour, vile as dust;
   All that flatters we disown:
   Righteousness is Thine alone.

2. Though we underwent for Thee
   Perils of the land and sea,
   Though we cast our lives away,
   Dying for Thee day by day,
   Boast we never of our own,
   Grace and strength are Thine alone.

3. Native cumberers of the ground,
   All our fruit from Thee is found;
   Grafted in Thine olive, Lord,
   New-begotten by Thy word,
   All we have is Thine alone:
   Life and power are not our own.

4. And when Thy returning voice
   Calls Thy faithful to rejoice,
   When the countless throng to Thee
   Cast their crowns of victory,
   We will sing before the Throne,
   "Thine the glory, not our own!"

124 S. M.

"The precious blood of Christ, as of a lamb without blemish."

1. NOT all the blood of beasts
   On Jewish altars slain,
Could give the guilty conscience peace,
   Or wash away the stain.

2. But Christ, the heavenly Lamb,
   Takes all our sins away,
A sacrifice of nobler name
   And richer blood than they.

3. My faith would lay her hand
   On that dear head of Thine,
While like a penitent I stand,
   And there confess my sin.

4. My soul looks back to see
   The burdens Thou didst bear,
When hanging on the cursèd tree,
   And hopes her guilt was there.

5. Believing, we rejoice
   To see the curse remove;
We bless the Lamb with cheerful voice,
   And sing His dying love.

125 C. M.

"In that day there shall be a fountain opened . . . for sin and for uncleanness."

1. THERE is a fountain filled with blood
   Drawn from Immanuel's veins;
And sinners, plunged beneath that flood,
   Lose all their guilty stains.

2. The dying thief rejoiced to see
    That fountain in his day ;
  And there have I, as vile as he,
    Washed all my sins away.

3. Dear dying Lamb! Thy precious blood
    Shall never lose its power,
  Till all the ransomed Church of God
    Be saved, to sin no more.

4. E'er since, by faith, I saw the stream
    Thy flowing wounds supply,
  Redeeming love has been my theme,
    And shall be till I die.

5. Then, in a nobler, sweeter song,
    I'll sing Thy power to save,
  When this poor lisping, stammering tongue
    Lies silent in the grave.

6. Lord, I believe Thou hast prepared,
    Unworthy though I be,
  For me a blood-bought free reward,
    A golden harp for me ;

7. 'Tis strung, and tuned for endless years,
    And formed by power divine,
  To sound, in God the Father's ears,
    No other name but Thine.

126   **8, 6.**

*" Behold the Lamb of God, which taketh
    away the sin of the world."*

1. JUST as I am, without one plea,
    But that Thy blood was shed for me,
    And that Thou bidd'st me come to Thee,
    O Lamb of God, I come!

2. Just as I am, and waiting not
   To rid my soul of one dark blot,
   To Thee, whose blood can cleanse each spot,
     O Lamb of God, I come!

3. Just as I am, though tossed about
   With many a conflict, many a doubt,
   Fightings and fears within, without,
     O Lamb of God, I come!

4. Just as I am, poor, wretched, blind;
   Sight, riches, healing of the mind,
   Yea, all I need, in Thee to find,
     O Lamb of God, I come!

5. Just as I am, Thou wilt receive,
   Wilt welcome, pardon, cleanse, relieve!
   Because Thy promise I believe,
     O Lamb of God, I come!

6. Just as I am (Thy love unknown
   Has broken every barrier down),
   Now to be Thine, yea, Thine alone,
     O Lamb of God, I come!

7. Just as I am, of that free love
   The breadth, length, depth, and height to prove,
   Here for a season, then above,
     O Lamb of God, I come!

127   **7, 6.**

" Cast thy burden upon the Lord."

1. I LAY my sins on Jesus,
     The spotless Lamb of God;
   He bears them all, and frees us
     From the accursèd load.

I bring my guilt to Jesus,
  To wash my crimson stains
White in His blood most precious,
  Till not a spot remains.

2. I lay my wants on Jesus,
  All fulness dwells in Him ;
He heals all my diseases,
  He doth my soul redeem.
I lay my griefs on Jesus,
  My burdens and my cares ;
He from them all releases,
  He all my sorrows shares.

3. I rest my soul on Jesus,
  This weary soul of mine ;
His right hand me embraces,
  I on His breast recline.
I love the name of Jesus,
  Immanuel, Christ, the Lord ;
Like fragrance on the breezes,
  His name abroad is poured.

4. I long to be like Jesus,
  Meek, loving, lowly, mild ;
I long to be like Jesus,
  The Father's Holy Child ;
I long to be with Jesus,
  Amid the heavenly throng ;
To sing with saints His praises,
  To learn the angels' song.

128   **7s.**

" That Rock was Christ."

1. ROCK of Ages, cleft for me,
  Let me hide myself in Thee ;
Let the water and the blood,
From Thy riven side which flowed,

Be of sin the double cure,
Cleanse me from its guilt and power.

2. Not the labours of my hands
Can fulfil Thy law's demands;
Could my zeal no respite know,
Could my tears for ever flow,
All for sin could not atone;
Thou must save, and Thou alone.

3. Nothing in my hand I bring;
Simply to Thy cross I cling;
Naked, come to Thee for dress;
Helpless, look to Thee for grace;
Foul, I to the fountain fly:
Wash me, Saviour, or I die.

4. While I draw this fleeting breath,
When my eyelids close in death,
When I soar through tracts unknown,
See Thee on Thy judgment-throne;
Rock of Ages, cleft for me,
Let me hide myself in Thee.

129   7s.

*" A man shall be as an hiding-place from
the wind, and a covert from the tempest."*

1. JESUS, Lover of my soul,
Let me to Thy bosom fly,
While the nearer waters roll,
While the tempest still is high.

2. Hide me, O my Saviour, hide,
Till the storm of life is past;
Safe into the haven guide;
O receive my soul at last!

3. Other refuge have I none;
    Hangs my helpless soul on Thee;
Leave, ah! leave me not alone;
    Still support and comfort me.

4. All my trust on Thee is stayed,
    All my help from Thee I bring;
Cover my defenceless head
    With the shadow of Thy wing.

5. Thou, O Christ, art all I want;
    More than all in Thee I find:
Raise the fallen, cheer the faint,
    Heal the sick, and lead the blind.

6. Just and holy is Thy name;
    I am all unrighteousness:
False and full of sin I am;
    Thou art full of truth and grace.

7. Plenteous grace with Thee is found,
    Grace to cover all my sin;
Let the healing streams abound;
    Make and keep me pure within.

8. Thou of life the fountain art,
    Freely let me take of Thee;
Spring Thou up within my heart,
    Rise to all eternity.

130   6, 4.

" Be not afraid, only believe."

1. My faith looks up to Thee,
Thou Lamb of Calvary,
    Saviour divine:
Now hear me while I pray;

Take all my guilt away;
O let me from this day
　　Be wholly Thine!

2. May Thy rich grace impart
Strength to my fainting heart,
　　My zeal inspire;
As Thou hast died for me,
O may my love to Thee
Pure, warm, and changeless be,
　　A living fire.

3. While life's dark maze I tread,
And griefs around me spread,
　　Be Thou my guide;
Bid darkness turn to day,
Wipe sorrow's tears away,
Nor let me ever stray
　　From Thee aside.

4. When ends life's transient dream,
When death's cold sullen stream
　　Shall o'er me roll,
Blest Saviour, then, in love,
Fear and distrust remove;
O bear me safe above,
　　A ransomed soul.

131　　　　　　　　　　　　6, 4.

*"If we confess our sins, he is faithful
and just to forgive."*

1. No; not despairingly
　　Come I to Thee!
No; not distrustingly
　　Bend I the knee!
Sin hath gone over me,
Yet is this still my plea,
　　Jesus hath died.

2. Lord, I confess to Thee
    Sadly my sin;
All I am, tell I Thee;
    All I have been!
Purge Thou my sin away,
Wash Thou my soul this day,
    Lord, make me clean!

3. Faithful and just art Thou
    Forgiving all;
Loving and kind art Thou
    When poor ones call;
Lord, let the cleansing blood,
Blood of the Lamb of God,
    Pass o'er my soul!

4. Then all is peace and light
    This soul within;
Thus shall I walk with Thee,
    Loved though unseen;
Leaning on Thee, my God,
Guided along the road,
    Nothing between!

132 C. M.

" *Who will have all men to be saved,
and to come unto the knowledge of
the truth.*"

1. GOD loved the world of sinners lost
    And ruined by the fall;
Salvation full, at highest cost,
    He offers free to all.

Oh, 'twas love, 'twas wondrous love!
    The love of God to me;
It brought my Saviour from above,
    To die on Calvary.

2. E'en now by faith I claim Him mine,
   The risen Son of God;
Redemption by His death I find,
   And cleansing through the blood.

3. Love brings the glorious fulness in,
   And to His saints makes known
The blessed rest from inbred sin,
   Through faith in Christ alone.

4. Believing souls, rejoicing go;
   There shall to you be given
A glorious foretaste, here below,
   Of endless life in heaven.

5. Of victory now o'er Satan's power
   Let all the ransomed sing,
And triumph in the dying hour
   Through Christ the Lord our King.

133   10S.

*"Jesus, thou Son of David, have mercy
on me."*

1. JESUS, Thou Son of David, hear my cry!
For I am blind, and full of misery.
Mercy is Thine; have mercy, Lord, on me!
Touch Thou mine eyes, O give me now to
      see!

2. Sin is my blindness, Lord, sin my disease;
Sin veils my heart, sin robs my soul of peace;
Sin keeps me back from loving sight of Thee;
Have mercy, Lord, from sin, O set me free!

3. I do not see Thee, Jesus! but they say
That Thou art passing by—art in the way:

'Tis true! the sound of Thy blest footsteps
near,
And accents of Thy voice, O Lord, I hear.

4. O loving voice! it calls out, "Come to me!"
It asks, "What wouldst thou I should do to
thee?"
Jesus, Thou Son of David, shed Thy light
O'er my dark soul, and say, "Receive thy
sight!"

5. What Thou hast done for others, I believe,
Lord, Thou wilt do for me! I shall receive
My sight!—shall see Thee, Jesus, face to face,
In all Thy might of majesty and grace.

6. My cry is heard! Thy mighty, loving hand
Has touched my inner eye; at Thy command,
The dark'ning scales have fallen from my heart,
And now I see Thee, Jesus, as Thou art!

134   8, 7.

"Looking unto Jesus."

1. SWEET the moments, rich in blessing,
Which before the cross we spend,
Life, and health, and peace possessing,
From the sinner's dying Friend.
Here we rest, in wonder viewing
All our sins on Jesus laid,
Here we see redemption flowing
From the sacrifice He made.

2. Here we find the dawn of heaven,
While upon the cross we gaze,
See our trespasses forgiven,
And our songs of triumph raise,

Oh! that near the cross abiding,
  We may to the Saviour cleave,
Nought with Him our hearts dividing,
  All for Him content to leave.

135

*" Let us therefore come boldly unto the
throne of grace."*

1. APPROACH, my soul, the mercy-seat,
    Where Jesus answers prayer:
  There humbly fall before His feet,
    For none can perish there.

2. Thy promise is my only plea,
    With this I venture nigh:
  Thou callest burdened souls to Thee,
    And such, O Lord, am I.

3. Bowed down beneath a load of sin,
    By Satan sorely prest;
  By war without and fears within,
    I come to Thee for rest.

4. Be Thou my shield and hiding-place;
    That, shel'red near Thy side,
  I may my fierce accuser face,
    And tell him Thou hast died.

5. O wondrous love! to bleed and die,
    To bear the cross and shame,
  That guilty sinners such as I
    Might plead Thy gracious name!

136

7s.

" Whatsoever ye shall ask in my name,
that will I do."

1. COME, my soul, thy suit prepare,
Jesus loves to answer prayer;
He Himself has bid thee pray,
Therefore will not say thee nay.

2. Thou art coming to a King,
Large petitions with thee bring;
For His grace and power are such,
None can ever ask too much.

3. With my burden I begin:
Lord, remove this load of sin!
Let Thy blood, for sinners spilt,
Set my conscience free from guilt.

4. Lord, I come to Thee for rest;
Take possession of my breast;
There Thy blood-bought right maintain,
And without a rival reign.

5. While I am a pilgrim here,
Let Thy love my spirit cheer,
As my Guide, my Guard, my Friend,
Lead me to my journey's end.

137

L. M.

" I will commune with thee from above
the mercy-seat."

1. FROM every stormy wind that blows,
From every swelling tide of woes,
There is a calm, a sure retreat,
'Tis found beneath the mercy-seat.

2. There is a place, where Jesus sheds
   The oil of gladness on our heads,
   A place than all besides more sweet,
   The blood-besprinkled mercy-seat.

3. There is a scene, where spirits blend,
   Where friend holds fellowship with friend :
   Though sundered far, by faith they meet
   Around one common mercy-seat.

4. Ah! whither could we flee for aid,
   When tempted, desolate, dismayed?
   Or how the hosts of hell defeat,
   Had suffering saints no mercy-seat?

5. O let my hand forget her skill,
   My tongue be silent, cold, and still,
   This bounding heart forget to beat,
   If I forget Thy mercy-seat.

138   8s.

" Tell me, I pray thee, thy name."

1. COME, O Thou Traveller unknown,
   Whom still I hold, but cannot see ;
   My company before is gone,
   And I am left alone with Thee ;
   With Thee all night I mean to stay,
   And wrestle till the break of day.

2. In vain Thou strugglest to get free,
   I never will unloose my hold ;
   Art Thou the Man that died for me?
   The secret of Thy love unfold :
   Wrestling, I will not let Thee go,
   Till I Thy name, Thy nature know.

3. Wilt Thou not yet to me reveal
    Thy new, unutterable name ?
Tell me, I still beseech Thee, tell ;
    To know it now, resolved I am :
Wrestling, I will not let Thee go
Till I Thy name, Thy nature know.

4. I know Thee, Saviour, who Thou art,
    Jesus, the feeble sinner's Friend ;
Nor wilt Thou with the night depart,
    But stay and love me to the end :
Thy mercies never shall remove ;
Thy nature and Thy name is Love.

5. The Sun of righteousness on me
    Hath risen with healing in His wings ;
Withered my nature's strength, from Thee
    My soul its life and succour brings ;
My help is all laid up above ;
Thy nature and Thy name is Love.

139

P. M.

*" I will not let thee go, except thou bless
me."*

1. I WILL not let Thee go, Thou Help in time of
    need !
  Heap ill on ill, I trust Thee still,
E'en when it seems that Thou wouldst slay in-
    deed !
    Do as Thou wilt with me ;
    I yet will cling to Thee ;
Hide Thou Thy face, yet, Help in time of need,
    I will not let Thee go !

2. I will not let Thee go ; should I forsake my
    bliss ?
  No, Lord, Thou'rt mine, and I am Thine ;

Thee will I hold when all things else I miss.
　　Though dark and sad the night,
　　Joy cometh with Thy light,
O Thou, my Sun; should I forsake my bliss?
　　I will not let Thec go!

3. I will not let Thee go, my God, my Life, my
　　　　Lord!
　　Not death can tear me from His care,
Who for my sake His soul in death outpoured.
　　Thou diedst in love to me;
　　I say, in love to Thee,
E'en when my heart shall break, my Life, my
　　　Lord,
　　I will not let Thee go!

140　　　　　　　　　　8, 7.

" There shall be showers of blessing."

1. LORD, I hear of showers of blessing
　　Thou art scattering, full and free—
Showers, the thirsty land refreshing;
　　Let some drops descend on me.

2. Pass me not, O gracious Father,
　　Sinful though my heart may be;
Thou might'st leave me, but the rather
　　Let Thy mercy light on me.

3. Pass me not, O tender Saviour;
　　Let me live and cling to Thee;
For I'm longing for Thy favour;
　　Whilst Thou'rt calling, O call me.

4. Pass me not, O mighty Spirit!
　　Thou canst make the blind to see:
Witnesser of Jesus' merit!
　　Speak the word of power to me.

5. Love of God, so pure and changeless;
   Blood of Christ, so rich, so free;
   Grace of God, so strong and boundless —
   Magnify them all in me.

141.   S. M.

" Revive thy work in the midst of the years."

1. REVIVE Thy work, O Lord !
   Thy mighty arm make bare ;
Speak with the voice which wakes the dead,
   And make Thy people hear.
   Revive Thy work, O Lord !
   Disturb this sleep of death,
Quicken the smouldering embers, now,
   By Thine almighty breath !

2. Revive Thy work, O Lord !
   Create soul-thirst for Thee,
And hungering for the bread of life
   O may our spirits be.
   Revive Thy work, O Lord !
   Exalt the Saviour's name ;
And by the Holy Ghost, our love
   For Thee and Thine inflame.

3. Revive Thy work, O Lord !
   Give power unto Thy word ;
Grant that Thy blessed gospel may
   In living faith be heard.
   Revive Thy work, O Lord !
   Give pentecostal showers :
The glory shall be all Thy own,
   The blessing, Lord, be ours !

142 C. M.

" Lord, help me."

1. O HELP us, Lord! each hour of need,
   Thy heavenly succour give;
Help us in thought, and word, and deed,
   Each hour on earth we live.

2. O help us when our spirits bleed
   With contrite anguish sore;
And when our hearts are cold and dead,
   O help us, Lord, the more.

3. O help us, through the prayer of faith,
   More firmly to believe;
For still, the more the servant hath,
   The more shall he receive.

4. O help us, Jesus, from on high;
   We know no help but Thee;
O help us so to live and die,
   As Thine in heaven to be.

143 L. M.

" The Lord is my light, and my salvation."

1. ETERNAL Beam of Light Divine,
   Fountain of unexhausted love,
In whom the Father's glories shine,
   Through earth beneath and heaven above:

2. Jesus! the weary wanderer's Rest!
   Give me Thy easy yoke to bear;
With steadfast patience arm my breast,
   With spotless love and lowly fear.

3. Be Thou, O Rock of Ages, nigh!
   So shall each murmuring thought be gone:

And grief, and fear, and care shall fly
As clouds before the mid-day sun.

4. Speak to my warring passions peace;
Say to my trembling heart, Be still:
Thy power my strength and fortress is,
For all things serve Thy sovereign will.

144   8, 7.

*" There is a friend that sticketh closer
than a brother."*

1. WHAT a Friend we have in Jesus,
All our sins and griefs to bear!
What a privilege to carry
Every thing to God in prayer!
O what peace we often forfeit,
O what needless pain we bear,
All because we do not carry
Every thing to God in prayer!

2. Have we trials and temptations?
Is there trouble anywhere?
We should never be discouraged;
Take it to the Lord in prayer.
Can we find a friend so faithful,
Who will all our sorrows share?
Jesus knows our every weakness;
Take it to the Lord in prayer.

3. Are we weak and heavy-laden,
Cumbered with a load of care?
Precious Saviour, still our refuge,
Take it to the Lord in prayer.
Do thy friends despise, forsake thee?
Take it to the Lord in prayer;
In His arms He'll take and shield thee;
Thou wilt find a solace there.

145 C. M.

*" When he had sent the multitudes away,
he went up into a mountain, apart, to
pray."*

1. FAR from the world, O Lord, I flee,
    From strife and tumult far,
  From scenes where Satan wages still
    His most successful war.

2. The calm retreat, the silent shade,
    With prayer and praise agree,
  And seem, by Thy sweet bounty, made
    For those who follow Thee.

3. There, if Thy Spirit touch the soul,
    And grace her mean abode,
  O with what peace and joy and love
    She communes with her God!

4. Author and guardian of my life,
    Sweet source of light divine,
  And — all harmonious names in one —
    My Saviour, Thou art mine.

146 C. M.

*" Remember thou me, for thy goodness'
sake, O Lord."*

1. O THOU, from whom all goodness flows,
    I lift my heart to Thee;
  In all my sorrows, conflicts, woes,
    Good Lord, remember me.

2. When groaning on my burdened heart
    My sins lie heavily,
  My pardon speak, new peace impart,
    In love remember me.

3. Temptations sore obstruct my way,
   And ills I cannot flee;
   O give me strength, Lord, as my day;
   For good remember me.

4. Distressed with pain, disease, and grief,
   This feeble body see;
   Grant patience, rest, and kind relief;
   Hear and remember me.

5. If on my face, for Thy dear name,
   Shame and reproaches be,
   All hail reproach, and welcome shame,
   If Thou remember me.

6. The hour is near; consigned to death,
   I own the just decree;
   Saviour, with my last parting breath,
   I'll cry, " Remember me."

147   8, 4.

*" The sacrifices of God are a broken
spirit."*

1. THERE is a holy sacrifice,
   Which God in heaven will not despise,
   Yea, which is precious in His eyes, —
   　　　The contrite heart.

2. That lofty One, before whose throne
   The countless hosts of heaven bow down,
   Another dwelling-place will own, —
   　　　The contrite heart.

3. The Holy One, the Son of God,
   His pardoning love will shed abroad,
   And consecrate as His abode
   　　　The contrite heart.

4. The Holy Spirit from on high
Will listen to its faintest sigh,
And cheer, and bless, and purify
          The contrite heart.

5. Saviour, I cast my hopes on Thee;
Such as Thou art, I fain would be;
In mercy, Lord, bestow on me
          The contrite heart.

148   8, 7.

" Out of the depths have I cried unto
thee, O Lord."

1. FROM depths of woe I raise to Thee
The voice of lamentation;
Lord, turn a gracious ear to me,
And hear my supplication:
If Thou shouldst be extreme to mark
Each secret sin and misdeed dark,
Oh! who could stand before Thee?

2. To wash away the crimson stain,
Grace, grace alone availeth;
Our works, alas! are all in vain,
In much the best life faileth:
No man can glory in Thy sight,
All must alike confess Thy might,
And live alone by mercy.

3. Therefore my trust is in the Lord,
And not in mine own merit;
On Him my soul shall rest, His word
Upholds my fainting spirit.
His promised mercy is my fort,
My comfort and my sweet support;
I wait for it with patience.

4. What though I wait the livelong night,
   And till the dawn appeareth?
   My heart still trusteth in His might,
   It doubteth not, nor feareth:
   So let the Israelite in heart,
   Born of the Spirit, do his part,
   And wait till God appeareth.

5. Although our sin is great indeed,
   God's mercies far exceed it;
   His hand can give the help we need,
   However much we need it:
   He is the Shepherd of the sheep,
   Who Israel doth guard and keep,
   And shall from sin redeem him.

149

7s.

" Jesus, Master, have mercy on us."

1. SAVIOUR, when in dust to Thee
   Low we bend the adoring knee;
   When repentant to the skies
   Scarce we lift our weeping eyes;
   Oh! by all the pains and woe
   Suffered once for man below,
   Bending from Thy throne on high,
   Hear our solemn litany!

2. By Thy helpless infant years,
   By Thy life of want and tears,
   By Thy days of sore distress
   In the savage wilderness;
   By the dread mysterious hour
   Of the insulting tempter's power;
   Turn, O turn a favouring eye,
   Hear our solemn litany!

3. By the sacred griefs that wept
O'er the grave where Lazarus slept;
By the boding tears that flowed
Over Salem's loved abode;
By the anguished sigh that told
Treachery lurked within Thy fold;
From Thy seat above the sky,
Hear our solemn litany!

4. By Thine hour of dire despair,
By Thine agony of prayer,
By the cross, the nail, the thorn,
Piercing spear, and torturing scorn,
By the gloom that veiled the skies
O'er the dreadful sacrifice,
Listen to our humble cry,
Hear our solemn litany!

5. By Thy deep expiring groan,
By the sad sepulchral stone,
By the vault, whose dark abode
Held in vain the rising God;
Oh! from earth to heaven restored,
Mighty re-ascended Lord,
Listen, listen to the cry
Of our solemn litany!

150   7s.

" Leaning upon her beloved."

1. SAVIOUR, more than life to me,
I am clinging close to Thee;
Let Thy precious blood applied
Keep me ever near Thy side.

Every day, every hour,
Let me feel Thy cleansing power:
May Thy tender love to me
Bind me closer, Lord, to Thee.

2. Through this changing world below
   Lead me gently, as I go;
   Trusting Thee, I cannot stray,
   I can never lose my way.

3. Let me love Thee more and more,
   Till this fleeting life is o'er;
   Till my soul is lost in love,
   In a brighter world above.

151   **7, 5, 8.**

*" Then hear thou in heaven thy dwelling-
place, and forgive."*

1. WHEN the weary, seeking rest,
     To Thy goodness flee;
   When the heavy-laden cast
     All their load on Thee;
   When the troubled, seeking peace,
     On Thy name shall call;
   When the sinner, seeking life,
     At Thy feet shall fall:
   Hear then, in love, O Lord, the cry,
   In heaven, Thy dwelling-place on high.

2. When the worldling, sick at heart,
     Lifts his soul above;
   When the prodigal looks back
     To His Father's love;
   When the proud man from his pride
     Stoops to seek Thy face;
   When the burdened brings his guilt
     To Thy throne of grace:
   Hear then, in love, O Lord, the cry,
   In heaven, Thy dwelling-place on high.

3. When the stranger asks a home,
     All his toils to end;
   When the hungry craveth food,
     And the poor a friend;

When the sailor on the wave
  Bows the fervent knee ;
When the soldier on the field
  Lifts his heart to Thee :
Hear then, in love, O Lord, the cry,
In heaven, Thy dwelling-place on high.

4. When the man of toil and care
  In the city crowd ;
When the shepherd on the moor
  Names the name of God ;
When the learnèd and the high,
  Tired of earthly fame,
Upon higher joys intent,
  Name the blessed name :
Hear then, in love, O Lord, the cry,
In heaven, Thy dwelling-place on high.

5. When the child, with grave fresh lip,
  Youth, or maiden fair ;
When the aged, weak and grey,
  Seek Thy face in prayer ;
When the widow weeps to Thee,
  Sad and lone and low ;
When the orphan brings to Thee
  All his orphan woe :
Hear then, in love, O Lord, the cry,
In heaven, Thy dwelling-place on high.

6. When creation, in her pangs,
  Heaves her heavy groan ;
When Thy Salem's exiled sons
  Breathe their bitter moan ;
When Thy waiting, weeping Church,
  Looking for a home,
Sendeth up her silent sigh,
  Come, Lord Jesus, come !
Hear then, in love, O Lord, the cry,
In heaven, Thy dwelling-place on high.

152   8, 7, 4.

" He will be our guide even unto death."

1. GUIDE me, O Thou great Jehovah!
    Pilgrim through this barren land:
   I am weak, but Thou art mighty;
    Hold me with Thy powerful hand.
        Bread of heaven!
    Feed me now and evermore!

2. Open now the crystal fountain,
    Whence the healing streams do flow;
   Let the fiery, cloudy pillar
    Lead me all my journey through.
        Strong Deliverer!
    Be Thou still my strength and shield!

3. When I tread the verge of Jordan,
    Bid my anxious fears subside;
   Death of death, and hell's destruction,
    Land me safe on Canaan's side.
        Songs of praises
    I will ever give to Thee!

153   L. M.

" Whosoever shall be ashamed of me, and
of my words, . . . of him also shall the
Son of man be ashamed."

1. JESUS! and shall it ever be,
   A mortal man ashamed of Thee,
   Ashamed of Thee, whom angels praise,
   Whose glories shine through endless days!

2. Ashamed of Jesus! just as soon
   Let midnight blush to think of noon;
   'Tis midnight with my soul till He,
   Bright Morning Star, bids darkness flee.

3. Ashamed of Jesus! that dear Friend
   On whom my hopes of heaven depend!
   No! when I blush, be this my shame,
   That I so feebly love His name.

4. Ashamed of Jesus! yes, I may,
   When I've no sins to wash away,
   No tear to wipe, no joy to crave,
   No fears to quell, no soul to save.

5. Till then — nor is my boasting vain —
   Till then, I boast a Saviour slain!
   And O may this my glory be,
   That Christ is not ashamed of me!

154

8, 7.

" Lo, we have left all, and followed thee."

1. JESUS, I my cross have taken,
   All to leave and follow Thee;
   Destitute, despised, forsaken,
   Thou from hence my all shalt be.

2. Go, then, earthly fame and treasure!
   Come disaster, scorn and pain!
   In Thy service, pain is pleasure,
   With Thy favour, loss is gain.

3. Man may trouble and distress me,
   'Twill but drive me to Thy breast;
   Life with trials hard may press me,
   Heaven will bring me sweeter rest.

4. O 'tis not in grief to harm me,
   While Thy love is left to me!
   O 'twere not in joy to charm me,
   Were that joy unmixed with Thee!

5. Take, my soul, thy full salvation;
   Rise o'er sin, and fear, and care;
Joy to find, in every station,
   Something still to do or bear.

6. Think what Spirit dwells within thee!
   What a Father's smile is thine!
What a Saviour died to win thee!
   Child of heaven, shouldst thou repine?

7. Haste, then, on from grace to glory,
   Armed by faith and winged by prayer;
Heaven's eternal day's before thee,
   God's own hand shall guide thee there.

8. Soon shall close thy earthly mission,
   Swift shall pass thy pilgrim days;
Hope soon change to glad fruition,
   Faith to sight, and prayer to praise.

155   S. M.

*" The sufferings of this present time are
not worthy to be compared with the
glory which shall be revealed in us."*

1. OH! what, if we are Christ's,
   Is earthly shame or loss?
Bright shall the crown of glory be
   When we have borne the cross.

2. Keen was the trial once,
   Bitter the cup of woe,
When martyred saints, baptized in blood,
   Christ's sufferings shared below.

3. Bright is their glory now,
   Boundless their joy above,
Where, on the bosom of their God,
   They rest in perfect love.

4. Lord, may that grace be ours,
   Like them in faith to bear
All th.t of sorrow, grief, or pain
   May be our portion here:

5. Enough, if Thou at last
   The word of blessing give,
And let us rest beneath Thy feet,
   Where saints and angels live.

6. All glory, Lord, to Thee,
   Whom heaven and earth adore;
To Father, Son, and Holy Ghost,
   One God for evermore.

156

L. M.

"My beloved is mine, and I am his."

1. O HAPPY day that fixed my choice
   On Thee, my Saviour and my God!
Well may this glowing heart rejoice,
   And tell its raptures all abroad.

2. 'Tis done; the great transaction's done;
   I am my Lord's, and He is mine.
He drew me, and I followed on,
   Charmed to confess the voice divine.

3. Now rest, my long-divided heart;
   Fixed on this blissful centre rest.
With ashes who would grudge to part,
   Wh :n called on angels' bread to feast?

4. High heaven, that heard the solemn vow,
   That vow renewed shall often hear;
Till in life's late:: hour I bow,
   And bless in death a bond so dear.

157   11, 10.

*" Whether we live, therefore, or die, we
are the Lord's."*

1. WE are the Lord's; His all-sufficient merit,
    Sealed on the cross, to us this grace accords;
We are the Lord's, and all things shall inherit;
    Whether we live or die, we are the Lord's.

2. We are the Lord's; then let us gladly tender
    Our souls to Him, in deeds, not empty words;
Let heart, and tongue, and life, combine to render
    No doubtful witness that we are the Lord's.

3. We are the Lord's; no darkness brooding o'er
    us
    Can make us tremble, while this star affords
A steady light along the path before us —
    Faith's full assurance that we are the Lord's.

4. We are the Lord's; no evil can befall us
    In the dread hour of life's fast loosening
    cords;
No pangs of death shall even then appall us;
    Death we shall vanquish, for we are the
    Lord's.

158   8, 7.

"Hitherto hath the Lord helped us."

1. COME, Thou Fount of every blessing!
    Tune my heart to sing Thy grace;
Streams of mercy never ceasing
    Call for songs of loudest praise.

2. With celestial fervour glowing,
    Let me sing like those above;
While my heart, with joy o'erflowing,
    Dwells on God's unchanging love.

3. Here I raise my Ebenezer,
      Hither by Thy help I'm come ;
    And I hope, by Thy good pleasure,
      Safely to arrive at home.

4. Jesus sought me when a stranger,
      Wandering from the fold of God ;
    He, to save my soul from danger,
      Interposed His precious blood.

5. Oh! to grace how great a debtor
      Daily I'm constrained to be !
    Let that grace, Lord, like a fetter
      Bind my wandering heart to Thee.

6. Prone to wander, Lord, I feel it,
      Prone to leave the God I love,
    Here's my heart, O take and seal it,
      Seal it from Thy courts above.

159   8s.

*" The love of Christ which passeth knowl-
edge."*

1. JESUS, Thy boundless love to me
      No thought can reach, no tongue declare;
    Oh ! bend my wayward heart to Thee,
      And reign without a rival there :
    Thine, wholly Thine, alone I'd live ;
    Myself to Thee entirely give.

2. O Lord, how gracious is Thy way,
      All fear before Thy presence flies ;
    Care, anguish, sorrow, pass away
      Where'er thy healing beams arise :
    Lord Jesus, nothing may I see,
    Nothing desire apart from Thee.

3. What in thy love possess I not?
   My star by night, my sun by day,
My spring of life when parched with drought,
   My wine to cheer, my bread to stay,
My strength, my shield, my safe abode,
My robe before the throne of God.

4. In suffering be Thy love my peace,
   In weakness be Thine arm my strength;
And when the storms of life shall cease,
   And Thou from heaven shalt come at length,
Lord Jesus, then this heart shall be
For ever satisfied with Thee.

160   6, 4.

" Whom, having not seen, ye love."

1. MORE love to Thee, O Christ,
   More love to Thee!
Hear Thou the prayer I make
   On bended knee;
This is my earnest plea:
More love, O Christ, to Thee,
   More love to Thee.

2. Once earthly joy I craved,
   Sought peace and rest,
Now Thee alone I seek,
   Give what is best:
This all my prayer shall be:
More love, O Christ, to Thee,
   More love to Thee.

3. Then shall my latest breath
   Whisper Thy praise;
This be the parting cry
   My heart shall raise,

This still its prayer shall be:
More love, O Christ, to Thee,
More love to Thee.

161   8, 7.

" God commendeth his love toward us."

1. LOVE Divine, all loves excelling,
      Joy of heaven, to earth come down!
   Fix in us Thy humble dwelling,
      All Thy faithful mercies crown.

2. Jesus, Thou art all compassion,
      Pure, unbounded love Thou art;
   Visit us with Thy salvation,
      Enter every trembling heart.

3. Come, almighty to deliver!
      Let us all Thy grace receive;
   Suddenly return, and never,
      Never more Thy temples leave:

4. Thee would we be always blessing,
      Serve Thee as Thy hosts above;
   Pray, and praise Thee without ceasing,
      Glory in Thy perfect love.

5. Finish, then, Thy new creation,
      Pure and spotless let us be;
   Let us see Thy great salvation,
      Perfectly restored in Thee.

6. Changed from glory into glory,
      Till in heaven we take our place,
   Till we cast our crowns before Thee,
      Lost in wonder, love, and praise.

162   **7, 6.**

" Your life is hid with Christ in God."

1. O LAMB of God! still keep me
   Near to Thy wounded side;
'Tis only there in safety
   And peace I can abide.
What foes and snares surround me!
   What lusts and fears within!
The grace that sought and found me
   Alone can keep me clean.

2. 'Tis only in Thee hiding,
   I know my life secure;
Only in Thee abiding,
   The conflict can endure:
Thine arm the vict'ry gaineth
   O'er every hurtful foe;
Thy love my heart sustaineth
   In all its cares and woe.

3. Soon shall my eyes behold Thee
   With rapture, face to face:
One half hath not been told me
   Of all Thy power and grace:
Thy beauty, Lord, and glory,
   The wonders of Thy love,
Shall be the endless story
   Of all Thy saints above.

163   **7, 5.**

*" My sheep hear my voice, and I know
them, and they follow me."*

1. JESUS, Shepherd of the sheep,
   Who Thy Father's flock dost keep,
Safe we wake and safe we sleep,
   Guarded still by Thee.

2. In Thy promise firm we stand,
   None can pluck us from Thy hand,
   Speak — we hear — at Thy command,
   We will follow Thee.

3. By Thy blood our souls were bought,
   By Thy life salvation wrought,
   By Thy light our feet are taught,
   Lord, to follow Thee.

4. Father, draw us to Thy Son,
   We with joy will follow on,
   Till the work of grace is done,
   And from sin set free,

5. We in robes of glory drest,
   Join the assembly of the blest,
   Gathered to eternal rest,
   In the fold with Thee.

164   C. M.

" Let this mind be in you which was
also in Christ Jesus."

1. LORD, as to Thy dear cross we flee
   And plead to be forgiven,
   So let Thy life our pattern be,
   And form our souls for heaven.

2. Help us, through good report and ill,
   Our daily cross to bear,
   Like Thee, to do our Father's will,
   Our brethren's griefs to share.

3. Let grace our selfishness expel,
   Our earthliness refine,
   And kindness in our bosoms dwell,
   As free and true as Thine.

4. If joy shall at Thy bidding fly,
   And grief's dark day come on,
   We, in our turn, would meekly cry,
   "Father, Thy will be done!"

5. Should friends misjudge, or foes defame,
   Or brethren faithless prove,
   Then, like Thine own, be all our aim
   To conquer them by love.

6. Kept peaceful in the midst of strife,
   Forgiving and forgiven,
   O may we lead the pilgrim's life,
   And follow Thee to heaven.

165 C. M.

*"Inasmuch as ye have done it unto one
of the least of these my brethren,
ye have done it unto me."*

1. FOUNTAIN of good, to own Thy love,
   Our thankful hearts incline;
   What can we render, Lord, to Thee,
   When all the worlds are Thine?

2. But Thou hast needy brethren here,
   Partakers of Thy grace,
   Whose names Thou wilt Thyself confess
   Before the Father's face.

3. And in their accents of distress
   Thy pleading voice is heard;
   In them Thou may'st be clothed, and fed,
   And visited, and cheered.

4. Thy face with reverence and with love
   We in Thy poor would see;
   O may we minister to them,
   And in them, Lord, to Thee!

166 L. M.

*" The fire shall ever be burning upon
the altar, it shall not go out."*

1. O THOU who came t from above,
    The pure celestial fire to impart,
Kindle a flame of sacred love
    On the mean altar of my heart.

2. There let it for Thy glory burn
    With inextinguishable blaze,
And, trembling, to its source return
    In humble prayer and fervent praise.

3. Jesus, confirm my heart's desire
    To work, and speak, and think for Thee;
Still let me guard the holy fire,
    And still stir up Thy gift in me;

4. Ready for all Thy perfect will,
    My acts of faith and love repeat,
Til' death Thy endless mercies seal,
    And make the sacrifice complete.

167 C. M.

*" Compassed about with so great a cloud
of witnesses."*

1. GIVE me the wings of faith to rise
    Within the veil, and see
The saints above, how great their joys,
    How bright their glories be.

2. Once they were mourning here below,
    And poured forth cries and tears;
They wrestled hard, as we do now,
    With sins, and doubts, and fears,

3. I ask them whence their victory came
   They, with united breath,
Ascribe their conquest to the Lamb,
   Their triumph to His death.

4. They marked the footsteps that He trod,
   His zeal inspired their breast;
And, following their incarnate God,
   They gained the promised rest.

5. Our glorious Leader claims our praise
   For His own pattern given,
While the long cloud of witnesses
   Show the same path to heaven.

168   S. M.

*" Whether we live therefore, or die,
we are the Lord's."*

1. JESUS, I live to Thee,
      The loveliest and best;
   My life in Thee, Thy life in me,
      In Thy blest love I rest.

2. Jesus, I die to Thee,
      Whenever death shall come;
   To die in Thee is life to me
      In my eternal home.

3. Whether to live or die,
      I know not which is best;
   To live in Thee is bliss to me,
      To die is endless rest.

4. Living or dying, Lord,
      I ask but to be Thine;
   My life in Thee, Thy life in me,
      Makes heaven for ever mine.

169   7s.

" To me to live is Christ, and to die is gain."

1. CHRIST, of all my hopes the ground,
    Christ, the spring of all my joy,
Still in Thee may I be found,
    Still for Thee my powers employ.

2. Let Thy love my heart inflame;
    Keep Thy fear before my sight;
Be Thy praise my highest aim;
    Be Thy smile my chief delight.

3. Fountain of o'erflowing grace,
    Freely from Thy fulness give ·
Till I close my earthly race,
    Be it ' Christ for me to live!'

4. Firmly trusting in Thy blood,
    Nothing shall my heart confound;
Safely I shall pass the flood,
    Safely reach Immanuel's ground.

5. Thus, O thus, an entrance give
    To the land of cloudless sky:
Having known it 'Christ to live,'
    Let me know it 'gain to die.'

170   8, 5, 3.

*" If any man serve me, let him follow
me; and where I am, there shall
also my servant be."*

1. ART thou weary, art thou languid,
    Art thou sore distrest?
'Come to Me,' saith One, 'and coming,
    Be at rest.'

2. Hath He marks to lead me to Him,
   If He be my guide?
'In His feet and hands are wound-prints,
   And His side.'

3. Is there diadem, as monarch,
   That His brow adorns?
'Yea, a crown, in very surety,
   But of thorns !'

4. If I find Him, if I follow,
   What His guerdon here?
'Many a sorrow, many a labour,
   Many a tear.'

5. If I still hold closely to Him,
   What hath He at last?
'Sorrow vanquished, labour ended,
   Jordan past !'

6. If I ask Him to receive me,
   Will He say me nay?
'Not till earth, and not till heaven,
   Pass away !'

7. Finding, following, keeping, struggling,
   Is He sure to bless?
'Angels, martyrs, saints and prophets,
   Answer, Yes !'

171

L. M.

*"Man goeth forth unto his work, and to
his labour, until the evening."*

1. FORTH in Thy name, O Lord, I go,
My daily labour to pursue;
Thee, only Thee, resolved to know,
In all I think, or speak, or do.

2. The task Thy wisdom hath assigned,
    O let me cheerfully fulfil;
In all my works Thy presence find,
    And prove Thy acceptable will.

3. Thee may I set at my right hand,
    Whose eyes my inmost substance see;
And labour on at Thy command,
    And offer all my works to Thee.

4. Give me to bear Thy easy yoke,
    And every moment watch and pray,
And still to things eternal look,
    And hasten to Thy glorious day.

172   8, 7.

" God loveth a cheerful giver."

1. LORD, Thou lov'st the cheerful giver,
    Who with open heart and hand,
Blesses freely, as a river
    That refreshes all the land;
Grant us then the grace of giving
    With a spirit large and free,
That our life and all our living
    We may consecrate to Thee!

2. We are Thine, Thy mercy sought us,
    Found us in death's dreadful way,
To the fold in safety brought us
    Never more from Thee to stray.
Thine own life Thou freely gavest
    As an offering on the cross
For each sinner whom Thou savest
    From eternal shame and loss.

3. Blest by Thee with gifts and graces
    May we heed Thy Church's call;

Gladly in all times and places
  Give to Thee who givest all.
Thou hast bought us, and no longer
  Can we claim to be our own ;
Ever free, and ever stronger,
  We shall serve Thee, Lord, alone.

4. Saviour, Thou hast freely given
  All the blessings we enjoy,
Earthly store and bread of heaven,
  Love and peace without alloy;
Humbly now we bow before Thee,
  And our all to Thee resign,
For the Kingdom, Power, and Glory,
  Are, O Lord, for ever Thine.

173   C. M.

" My soul followeth hard after thee."

1. O FOR a closer walk with God,
  A calm and heavenly frame ;
A light to shine upon the road
  That leads me to the Lamb!

2. Where is the blessedness I knew
  When first I saw the Lord ?
Where is the soul-refreshing view
  Of Jesus and His word?

3. What peaceful hours I once enjoyed !
  How sweet their memory still!
But they have left an aching void
  The world can never fill.

4. Return, O Holy Dove, return,
  Sweet messenger of rest;
I hate the sins that made Thee mourn,
  And drove Thee from my breast.

5. The dearest idol I have known,
   Whate'er that idol be,
Help me to tear it from Thy throne,
And worship only Thee.

6. So shall my walk be close with God,
   Calm and serene my frame;
So purer light shall mark the road
   That leads me to the Lamb.

174   6, 4.

"My soul thirsteth for God."

1. NEARER, my God, to Thee,
      Nearer to Thee!
   E'en though it be a cross
      That raiseth me,
   Still all my song shall be,
   Nearer, my God, to Thee,
      Nearer to Thee!

2. Though, like the wanderer,
      The sun gone down,
   Darkness be over me,
      My rest a stone;
   Yet in my dreams I'd be
   Nearer, my God, to Thee,
      Nearer to Thee!

3. There let the way appear
      Steps unto heaven;
   All that Thou send'st to me,
      In mercy given;
   Angels to beckon me
   Nearer, my God, to Thee,
      Nearer to Thee!

4. Then with my waking thoughts
    Bright with Thy praise,
Out of my stony griefs
    Bethel I'll raise;
So by my woes to be
. Nearer, my God, to Thee,
    Nearer to Thee!

5. Or if on joyful wing
    Cleaving the sky,
Sun, moon, and stars forgot,
    Upward I fly,
Still all my song shall be,
Nearer, my God, to Thee,
    Nearer to Thee!

175   C. M.

" Restore unto me the joy of thy salvation."

1. O FOR a heart to praise my God,
    A heart from sin set free,
A heart that always feels Thy blood
    So freely shed for me!

2. A heart resigned, submissive, meek,
    My great Redeemer's throne;
Where only Christ is heard to speak,
    Where Jesus reigns alone:

3. A humble, lowly, contrite heart,
    Believing, true, and clean;
Which neither life nor death can part
    From Him that dwells within:

4. A heart in every thought renewed,
    And full of love divine;
Perfect, and right, and pure, and good,
    A copy, Lord, of Thine!

5. Thy nature, gracious Lord, impart;
  Come quickly from above;
Write Thy new name upon my heart,
  Thy new, best name of love.

176 S. M.

*"Blessed are the pure in heart, for they
shall see God."*

1. BLEST are the pure in heart,
  For they shall see our God,
The secret of the Lord is theirs,
  Their soul is Christ's abode.

2. The Lord who left the heavens,
  Our life and peace to bring;
To dwell in lowliness with men,
  Their pattern and their King; —

3. He to the lowly soul
  Doth still Himself impart,
And for His dwelling, and His throne,
  Chooseth the pure in heart.

4. Lord, we Thy presence seek;
  May ours this blessing be;
Give us a pure and lowly heart,
  A temple meet for Thee.

177 8, 6.

*" The love of Christ, which   eth know-
ledge."*

1. O LOVE Divine, how sweet Thou art!
When shall I find my willing heart
  All taken up by Thee?
I thirst, I faint, I die to prove
The greatness of redeeming love,
  The love of Christ to me !

2. Stronger His love than death or hell;
   Its riches are unsearchable;
      The first-born sons of light
   Desire in vain its depths to see;
   They cannot reach the mystery,
      The length, and breadth, and height.

3. God only knows the love of God:
   Oh that it now were shed abroad
      In this poor stony heart!
   For love I sigh, for love I pine:
   This only portion, Lord, be mine,
      Be mine this better part!

4. Oh that I could for ever sit
   With Mary at the Master's feet;
      Be this my happy choice:
   My only care, delight, and bliss,
   My joy, my heaven on earth, be this,
      To hear the Bridegroom's voice.

178 C. M.

*"God is the strength of my heart, and
my portion for ever."*

1. My heart is resting, O my God,
      I will give thanks and sing;
   My heart is at the secret source
      Of every precious thing.
   Now the frail vessel thou hast made
      No hand but Thine shall fill;
   For the waters of the earth have failed,
      And I am thirsty still.

2. I thirst for springs of heavenly life,
      And here all day they rise;
   I seek the treasure of Thy love,
      And close at hand it lies.

And a new song is in my mouth
    To long-loved music set;
Glory to Thee for all the grace
    I have not tasted yet.

3. Glory to Thee for strength withheld,
    For want and weakness known;
And the fear that sends me to Thyself
    For what is most my own.
I have a heritage of joy
    That yet I must not see;
But the hand that bled to make it mine
    Is keeping it for me.

4. My heart is resting, O my God,
    My heart is in Thy care;
I hear the voice of joy and health
    Resounding everywhere.
"Thou art my portion," saith my soul,
    Ten thousand voices say,
And the music of their glad Amen
    Will never die away.

179   8s.

" The unsearchable riches of Christ."

1. THOU hidden love of God, whose height,
    Whose depth unfathomed, no man knows,
I see from far Thy beauteous light,
    Inly I sigh for Thy repose :
My heart is pained, nor can it be
    At rest, till it finds rest in Thee.

2. 'Tis mercy all, that Thou hast brought
    My mind to seek its peace in Thee ;
Yet while I seek but find Thee not,
    No peace my wandering soul shall see.
O when shall all my wanderings end,
And all my steps to Thee-ward tend !

3. Is there a thing beneath the sun
   That strives with Thee my heart to share ?
Ah ! tear it thence, and reign alone,
   The Lord of every motion there.
Then shall my heart from earth be free,
When it hath found repose in Thee.

4. Each moment draw from earth away
   My heart that lowly waits Thy call ;
Speak to my inmost soul, and say,
   "I am Thy Saviour, God and All !"
To feel Thy power, to hear Thy voice,
To know Thy love, be all my choice.

180   S. M.

"When I awake, I am still with thee."

1. STILL with Thee, O my God,
   I would desire to be ;
By day, by night, at home, abroad,
   I would be still with Thee :

2. With Thee, when dawn comes in,
   And calls me back to care,
Each day returning to begin
   With Thee my God in prayer :

3. With Thee, amid the crowd
   That throngs the busy mart,
To hear Thy voice 'mid clamour loud,
   Speak softly to my heart :

4. With Thee, when day is done,
   And evening calms the mind ;
The setting, as the rising sun,
   With Thee my heart would find ;

5. With Thee, when darkness brings
The signal of repose ;
Calm in the shadow of Thy wings,
Mine eyelids I would close :

6. With Thee, in Thee, by faith
Abiding, I would be ;
By day, by night, in life, in death,
I would be still with Thee.

181

8, 4.

" Thy will be done."

1. My God and Father, while I stray
Far from my home on life's rough way,
O teach me from my heart to say,
'Thy will be done.'

2. Though dark my path and sad my lot,
Let me be still, and murmur not ;
But breathe the prayer divinely taught,
'Thy will be done.'

3. If Thou shouldst call me to resign
What most I prize — it ne'er was mine ;
I only yield Thee what is Thine ;
'Thy will be done.'

4. What though in lonely grief I sigh
For friends beloved no longer nigh ?
Submissive would I still reply,
'Thy will be done.'

5. Should pining sickness waste away
My life in premature decay :
My Father, still I'd strive to say,
'Thy will be done.'

6. If but my fainting heart be blessed
   With Thy free Spirit for its guest;
   My God, to Thee I leave the rest,—
       'Thy will be done.'

7. Renew my will from day to day;
   Blend it with Thine, and take away
   All that now makes it hard to say,
       'Thy will be done.'

8. Then, when on earth I breathe no more
   The prayer, oft mixed with tears before,
   I'll sing upon a happier shore,
       'Thy will be done.'

182   10s.

" Abide with us : for it is towards evening."

1. ABIDE with me ! fast falls the eventide ;
   The darkness deepens ; Lord, with me abide !
   When other helpers fail, and comforts flee,
   Help of the helpless, O abide with me !

2. Swift to its close ebbs out life's little day ;
   Earth's joys grow dim, its glories pass away ;
   Change and decay in all around I see :
   O Thou who changest not, abide with me !

3. Not a brief glance I beg, a passing word ;
   But as Thou dwell'st with Thy disciples, Lord,
   Familiar, condescending, patient, free,
   Come, not to sojourn, but abide, with me.

4. Come not in terrors, as the King of kings,
   But kind and good, with healing in Thy wings ;
   Tears for all woes, a heart for every plea :
   Come, Friend of sinners, thus abide with me.

5. Thou on my head in early youth didst smile;
And, though rebellious and perverse meanwhile,
Thou hast not left me, oft as I left Thee:
On to the close, O Lord, abide with me!

6. I need Thy presence every passing hour:
What but Thy grace can foil the tempter's
power?
Who like Thyself my guide and stay can be?
Through cloud and sunshine, O abide with me!

7. I fear no foe, with Thee at hand to bless;
Ills have no weight, and tears no bitterness:
Where is death's sting? where, grave, thy
victory?
I triumph still, if Thou abide with me.

8. Hold Thou Thy cross before my closing eyes,
Shine through the gloom, and point me to the
skies;
Heaven's morning breaks, and earth's vain
shadows flee:
In life, in death, O Lord, abide with me!

183   8, 7, 4.

*It is good that a man should both hope
and quietly wait for the salvation
of the Lord."*

1. WHATE'ER my God ordains is right:
Holy His will abideth;
I will be still, whate'er He doth,
And follow where He guideth.
He is my God;
Though dark my road,
He holds me that I shall not fall,
Wherefore to Him I leave it all.

2. Whate'er my God ordains is right:
   He never will deceive me;
He leads me by the proper path;
   I know He will not leave me,
      And take, content,
      What He hath sent:
His hand can turn my grief away,
And patiently I wait His day.

3. Whate'er my God ordains is right:
   Though now this cup in drinking
May bitter seem to my faint heart,
   I take it, all unshrinking:
      Tears pass away
      With dawn of day:
Sweet comfort yet shall fill my heart,
And pain and sorrow shall depart.

4. Whate'er my God ordains is right:
   Here shall my stand be taken;
Though sorrow, need, or death be mine,
   Yet am I not forsaken:
      My Father's care
      Is round me there:
He holds me that I shall not fall,
And so to Him I leave it all.

184   6s.

"Not my will, but thine, be done."

1. THY way, not mine, O Lord,
   However dark it be!
Lead me by Thine own hand,
   Choose out the path for me.
Smooth let it be or rough,
   It will be still the best,
Winding or straight, it leads
   Right onward to Thy rest.

2. I dare not choose my lot;
   I would not, if I might:
   Choose Thou for me, my God,
   So shall I walk aright.
   The kingdom that I seek
   Is Thine; so let the way
   That leads to it be Thine,
   Else I must surely stray.

3. Take Thou my cup, and it
   With joy or sorrow fill,
   As best to Thee may seem;
   Choose Thou my good and ill.
   Not mine, not mine the choice,
   In things or great or small;
   Be Thou my guide, my strength,
   My wisdom, and my all.

185
S. M.

" Commit thy way unto the Lord."

1. COMMIT thou all thy griefs
   And ways into His hands,
   To His sure truth and tender care,
   Who earth and heaven commands.

2. Who points the clouds their course,
   Whom winds and seas obey,
   He shall direct thy wandering feet,
   He shall prepare thy way.

3. Thou on the Lord rely;
   So safe shalt thou go on;
   Fix on His work thy steadfast eye,
   So shall thy work be done.

4. No profit canst thou gain
   By self-consuming care;

To Him commend thy cause; His ear
Attends the softest prayer.

5. Thy everlasting truth,
   Father! Thy ceaseless love,
Sees all Thy children's wants, and knows
   What best for each will prove.

6. And whatsoe'er Thou will'st
   Thou dost, O King of kings;
What Thy unerring wisdom chose
   Thy power to being brings.

7. When Thou arisest, Lord,
   Who shall Thy work withstand?
When all Thy children want Thou giv'st,
   Who, who shall stay Thy hand?

186

S. M.

" Wait on the Lord, be of good courage."

1. GIVE to the winds thy fears;
   Hope, and be undismayed:
God hears thy sighs and counts thy tears ·
   God shall lift up thy head.

2. Through waves, and clouds, and storms,
   He gently clears thy way;
Wait thou His time; so shall this night
   Soon end in joyous day.

3. What though thou rulest not?
   Yet heaven and earth and hell
Proclaim, God sitteth on the Throne,
   And ruleth all things well!

4. Leave to His sovereign sway
   To choose, and to command;

So shalt thou, wondering, own His way
How wise, how strong His hand;

5. Thou seest our weakness, Lord;
Our hearts are known to Thee;
O lift Thou up the sinking hand,
Confirm the feeble knee!

6. Let us, in life and death,
Thy steadfast truth declare,
And publish with our latest breath
Thy love a   guardian care.

187   8, 6.

" My soul is even as a weaned child."

1. FATHER, I know that all my life
Is portioned out for me;
And the changes that are sure to come
I do not fear to see;
But I ask Thee for a present mind,
Intent on pleasing Thee.

2. I ask Thee for a thoughtful love,
Through constant watching wise,
To meet the glad with joyful smiles,
And wipe the weeping eyes;
And a heart at leisure from itself,
To soothe and sympathise.

3. I would not have the restless will
That hurries to and fro,
Seeking for some great thing to do,
Or secret thing to know:
I would be treated as a child,
And guided where I go.

162

4. Wherever in the world I am,
    In whatsoe'er estate,
I have a fellowship with hearts
    To keep and cultivate;
And a work of lowly love to do
    For the Lord on whom I wait.

5. So I ask Thee for the daily strength,
    To none that ask denied;
And a mind to blend with outward life,
    While keeping at Thy side;
Content to fill a little space,
    If Thou be glorified.

6. And if some things I do not ask
    In my cup of blessing be;
I would have my spirit filled the more
    With grateful love to Thee;
More careful not to serve Thee much,
    But to please Thee perfectly.

7. There are briers besetting every path
    That call for patient care;
There is a cross in every lot,
    And an earnest need for prayer;
But a lowly heart that leans on Thee
    Is happy anywhere.

8. In a service which Thy love appoints
    There are no bonds for me;
For my inmost heart is taught the truth
    That makes Thy children free;
And a life of self-renouncing love
    Is a life of liberty.

188   S. M.

" My times are in thy hand."

1. My times are in Thy hand;
      My God, I wish them there.
   My life, my soul, my all, I leave
      Entirely to Thy care.

2. My times are in Thy hand,
      Whatever they may be;
   Pleasing or painful, dark or bright,
      As best may seem to Thee.

3. My times are in Thy hand,
      Why should I doubt or fear?
   A father's hand will never cause
      His child a needless tear.

4. My times are in Thy hand,
      I always trust in Thee;
   Till I possess the promised land,
      And all Thy glory see.

189   L. M.

" I am continually with thee."

1. O Thou, by long experience tried,
   Near whom no grief can long abide;
   My Lord! how full of sweet content
   I pass my years of banishment.

2. All scenes alike engaging prove,
   To souls impressed with sacred love:
   Where'er they dwell, they dwell in Thee;
   In heaven, in earth, or on the sea.

3. To me remains nor place nor time;
   My country is in every clime;
   I can be calm and free from care
   On any shore, since God is there.

4. While place we seek, or place we shun,
   The soul finds happiness in none;
   But with our God to guide our way,
   'Tis equal joy to go or stay.

190
C. M.

" Whether we live, therefore, or die, we are the Lord's."

1. LORD, it belongs not to my care
      Whether I die or live;
   To love and serve Thee is my share,
      And this Thy grace must give.

2. If life be long, I will be glad,
      That I may long obey;
   If short, yet why should I be sad
      To soar to endless day?

3. Come, Lord, when grace hath made me meet
      Thy blessèd face to see;
   For if Thy work on earth be sweet,
      What will Thy glory be?

4. Then I shall end my sad complaints,
      And weary sinful days,
   And join with the triumphant saints
      That sing Jehovah's praise.

5. My knowledge of that life is small,
      The eye of faith is dim;
   But 'tis enough that Christ knows all,
      And I shall be with Him.

191   6s.

"It is the Lord, let him do what seemeth him good."

1. My Saviour, as Thou wilt:
     O may Thy will be mine!
   Into Thy hand of love
     I would my all resign.
   Through sorrow, or through joy,
     Conduct me as Thine own,
   And help me still to say,
     My Lord, Thy will be done!

2. My Saviour, as Thou wilt:
     If needy here and poor,
   Give me Thy people's bread,
     Their portion rich and sure.
   The manna of Thy word
     Let my soul feed upon;
   And if all else should fail,
     My Lord, Thy will be done!

3. My Saviour, as Thou wilt:
     Though seen through many a tear,
   Let not my star of hope
     Grow dim or disappear.
   Since Thou on earth hast wept
     And sorrowed oft alone,
   If I must weep with Thee,
     My Lord, Thy will be done

4. My Saviour, as Thou wilt:
     All shall be well for me;
   Each changing future scene
     I gladly trust with Thee.
   Straight to my home above
     I travel calmly on,
   And sing in life or death,
     My Lord, Thy will be done!

*" He saith unto them, Why are ye so
fearful, O ye of little faith ?"*

1. BEGONE, unbelief,
      My Saviour is near,
   And for my relief
      Will surely appear.
   By prayer let me wrestle,
      And He will perform;
   With Christ in the vessel,
      I smile at the storm.

2. Though dark be my way,
      Since He is my guide,
   'Tis mine to obey,
      'Tis His to provide;
   Though cisterns be broken,
      And creatures all fail,
   The word He hath spoken
      Shall surely prevail.

3. His love in time past
      Forbids me to think
   He'll leave me at last
      In trouble to sink:
   Each sweet Ebenezer
      I have in review
   Confirms His good pleasure
      To help me quite through.

4. Since all that I meet
      Shall work for my good,
   The bitter is sweet,
      The medicine is food;
   Though painful at present,
      'Twill cease before long,
   And then, oh! how pleasant
      The conqueror's song!

*" Surely goodness and mercy shall follow
me all the days of my life."*

1. THOUGH troubles assail,
   And dangers affright,
Though friends should all fail,
   And foes all unite;
Yet one thing secures us,
   Whatever betide,
The Scripture assures us,
   'The Lord will provide.'

2. The birds, without barn
   Or storehouse, are fed;
From them let us learn
   To trust for our bread:
His saints what is fitting,
   Shall ne'er be denied,
So long as 'tis written,
   'The Lord will provide.

3. His call we obey,
   Like Abram of old,
Not knowing our way,
   But faith makes us bold;
For, though we are strangers
   We have a good guide,
And trust, in all dangers,
   'The Lord will provide.'

4. No strength of our own,
   Nor goodness we claim;
Yet since we have known
   The Saviour's great name,
In this our strong tower
   For safety we hide, —
The Lord is our power;
   'The Lord will provide.'

194

7s.

" The simplicity that is in Christ."

1. QUIET, Lord, my froward heart,
    Make me teachable and mild,
Upright, simple, free from art,
    Make me as a weanèd child:
From distrust and envy free,
Pleased with all that pleaseth Thee.

2. What Thou shalt to-day provide,
    Let me as a child receive;
What to-morrow may betide,
    Calmly to Thy wisdom leave;
'Tis enough that Thou wilt care,
Why should I the burden bear?

3. As a little child relies
    On a care beyond his own;
Knows he's neither strong nor wise;
    Fears to stir a step alone:
Let me thus with Thee abide,
As my Father, Guard, and Guide.

4. Thus preserved from Satan's wiles,
    Safe from dangers, free from fears,
May I live upon Thy smiles,
    Till the promised hour appears,
When the sons of God shall prove
All their Father's boundless love

195

8, 6.

*" In whom, though now ye see him not,
    yet believing, ye rejoice."*

1. O HOLY Saviour, Friend unseen,
The faint, the weak, on Thee may lean;
Help me, throughout life's varying scene,
    By faith to cling to Thee!

2. Blest with communion so divine,
   Take what Thou wilt, shall I repine,
   When, as the branches to the vine,
      My soul may cling to Thee?

3. Far from her home, fatigued, opprest,
   Here she has found a place of rest,
   An exile still, yet not unblest
      While she can cling to Thee!

4. Oft when I seem to tread alone
   Some barren waste with thorns o'ergrown,
   A voice of love, in gentlest tone,
      Whispers, 'Still cling to Me.'

5. Though faith and hope awhile be tried,
   I ask not, need not, aught beside:
   How safe, how calm, how satisfied,
      The soul that clings to Thee!

6. Blest is my lot, whate'er befall:
   What can disturb me, who appal,
   While, as my strength, my rock, my all,
      Saviour! I cling to Thee?

196   L. M.

*"I am poor and needy; yet the Lord
thinketh upon me."*

1. GOD of my life, to Thee I call;
   Afflicted at Thy feet I fall;
   When the great water-floods prevail,
   Leave not my trembling heart to fail.

2. Friend of the friendless and the faint,
   Where should I lodge my deep complaint?
   Where, but with Thee, whose open door
   Invites the helpless and the poor?

3. Did ever mourner plead with Thee,
   And Thou refuse that mourner's plea?
   Does not the word still fixed remain,
   That none shall seek Thy face in vain?

4. Poor though I am, despised, forgot,
   Yet God, my God, forgets me not;
   And he is safe, and must succeed,
   For whom the Lord vouchsafes to plead.

197   1Os.

" Return unto thy rest, O my soul."

1. BE still, my soul; the Lord is on thy side;
   Bear patiently thy cross of grief and pain;
   Leave to thy God to order and provide;
   In every change He faithful will remain.
   Be still, my soul; thy best, thy heavenly Friend
   Through thorny ways leads to a joyful end.

2. Be still, my soul; thy God doth undertake
   To guide the future as He has the past.
   Thy hope, thy confidence, let nothing shake;
   All now mysterious shall be bright at last.
   Be still, my soul; the waves and winds shall
        know
   His voice who ruled them while He dwelt below.

3. Be still, my soul; when dearest friends depart,
   And all is darkened in the vale of tears,
   Then thou shalt better know His love, His
        heart,
   Who comes to soothe thy sorrow and thy fears.
   Be still, my soul; thy Jesus can repay
   From His own fulness all He takes away.

171

4. Be still, my soul; the hour is hastening on
    When we shall be for ever with the Lord;
When disappointment, grief, and fear are gone,
    Sorrow forgot, love's purest joys restored.
Be still, my soul; when change and tears are
        past,
All safe and blessed we shall meet at last.

198   L. M.

*" He calleth his own sheep by name, and
leadeth them out."*

1. HE leadeth me! O blessed thought!
   O words with heavenly comfort fraught!
   Whate'er I do, where'er I be,
   Still 'tis God's hand that leadeth me.

        He leadeth me! He leadeth me!
        By His own hand He leadeth me;
        His faithful follower I would be,
        For by His hand He leadeth me.

2. Sometimes 'mid scenes of deepest gloom,
   Sometimes where Eden's bowers bloom,
   By waters calm, o'er troubled sea,
   Still 'tis His hand that leadeth me.

3. Lord, I would clasp Thy hand in mine,
   Nor ever murmur nor repine,
   Content, whatever lot I see,
   Since 'tis my God that leadeth me.

4. And when my task on earth is done,
   When, by Thy grace, the victory's won,
   E'en death's cold wave I will not flee,
   Since Thou through Jordan leadest me.

199 C. M.

" Be thankful unto him, and bless his name."

1. WHEN I survey life's varied scene,
   Amid the darkest hours,
   Sweet rays of comfort shine between,
   And thorns are mixed with flowers.

2. Lord, teach me to adore Thy hand,
   From whence my comforts flow,
   And let me in this desert land
   A glimpse of Canaan know.

3. And O, whate'er of earthly bliss
   Thy sovereign will denies,
   Accepted at Thy throne of grace,
   Let this petition rise:

4. Give me a calm, a thankful heart,
   From every murmur free;
   The blessings of Thy grace impart,
   And let me live to Thee.

5. Let the sweet hope that Thou art mine
   My path of life attend;
   Thy presence through my journey shine,
   And bless its happy end.

200 10, 4.

*" O send out thy light, and thy truth;
let them lead me."*

1. LEAD, kindly Light, amid the encircling gloom,
   Lead Thou me on;
   The night is dark, and I am far from home,
   Lead Thou me on;
   Keep Thou my feet; I do not ask to see
   The distant scene; one step enough for me.

2. I was not ever thus, nor prayed that Thou
Shouldst lead me on;
I loved to choose and see my path; but now
Lead Thou me on:
I loved the garish day, and, spite of fears,
Pride ruled my will: remember not past years.

3. So long Thy power hath blest me, sure it still
Will lead me on,
O'er moor and fen, o'er crag and torrent, till
The night is gone,
And with the morn those angel faces smile,
Which I have loved long since, and lost awhile.

201

C. M.

"I will bless the Lord at all times."

1. THROUGH all the changing scenes of life,
In trouble and in joy,
The praises of my God shall still
My heart and tongue employ.

2. The hosts of God encamp around
The dwellings of the just;
Deliverance He affords to all,
Who on His succour trust.

3. Oh, make but trial of His love,
Experience will decide,
How blest are they, and only they,
Who in His truth confide.

4. Fear Him, ye saints, and you will then
Have nothing else to fear;
Make you His service your delight,
Your wants shall be His care.

5. For God preserves the souls of those
   Who on His truth depend,
To them and their posterity
   His blessings shall descend.

202   7s.

If ye endure chastening, God dealeth
with you as with sons ; for what son
is he whom the father chasteneth
not ? "

1. 'TIS my happiness below,
     Not to live without the cross,
But the Saviour's power to know,
     Sanctifying every loss.

2. Trials must and will befall;
     But with humble faith to see
Love inscribed upon them all,
     This is happiness to me.

3. Trials make the promise sweet;
     Trials give new life to prayer;
Trials bring me to His feet,
     Lay me low and keep me there.

4. Did I meet no trials here,
     No correction by the way,
Might I not, with reason, fear
     I should prove a castaway?

5. Aliens may escape the rod,
     Sunk in earthly vain delight;
But the true-born child of God
     Must not, would not, if he might.

203 L. M.

*" I will mention the loving-kindnesses
of the Lord."*

1. AWAKE, my soul, in joyful lays,
To sing thy great Redeemer's praise!
He justly claims a song from me;—
His loving-kindness, O how free!

2. He saw me ruined in the Fall,
Yet loved me, notwithstanding all;
He saved me from my lost estate;—
His loving-kindness, O how great!

3. Though numerous hosts of mighty foes,
Though earth and hell my way oppose,
He safely leads my soul along;—
His loving-kindness, O how strong!

4. When trouble, like a gloomy cloud,
Has gathered thick, and thundered loud,
He near my soul has always stood;—
His loving-kindness, O how good!

5. Often I feel my sinful heart
Prone from my Saviour to depart;
But though I have Him oft forgot,
His loving-kindness changes not.

6. Soon shall I pass the gloomy vale;
Soon all my mortal powers must fail;
O may my last expiring breath
His loving-kindness sing in death!

7. Then let me mount and soar away,
To the bright world of endless day;
And sing with rapture and surprise
His loving-kindness in the skies.

204   **8s.**

*" I have loved thee with an everlasting
love."*

1. Now I have found the ground wherein
   Sure my soul's anchor may remain :
The wounds of Jesus, for my sin,
   Before the world's foundation slain ;
Whose mercy shall unshaken stay,
When heaven and earth are fled away.

2. O Love, thou bottomless abyss !
   My sins are swallowed up in Thee ;
Covered is my unrighteousness,
   Nor spot of guilt remains on me :
While Jesus' blood through earth and skies,
Mercy, free boundless mercy, cries.

3. With faith I plunge me in this sea ;
   Here is my hope, my joy, my rest ;
Hither, when hell assails, I flee ;
   I look into my Saviour's breast :
Away, sad doubt, and anxious fear !
Mercy is all that's written there.

4. Fixed on this ground will I remain,
   Though my heart fail and flesh decay ;
This anchor shall my soul sustain,
   When earth's foundations melt away:
Mercy's full power I then shall prove
Loved with an everlasting love.

205   **8, 7, 4.**

*" I give unto them eternal life, and they
shall never perish."*

1. SOVEREIGN grace ! o'er sin abounding,
   Ransomed souls the tidings swell ;

'Tis a deep that knows no sounding—
Who its breadth or length can tell?
On its glories
Let my soul for ever dwell!

2. What from Christ the soul can sever,
Bound by everlasting bands?
Once in Him, in Him for ever,
Thus the eternal covenant stands,
None shall pluck thee
From the Strength of Israel's hands.

3. Heirs of God, joint-heirs with Jesus,
Long ere time its race began,
To His name eternal praises!
O what wonders love hath done!
One with Jesus,
By eternal union one.

4. On such love, my soul, still ponder,
Love so great, so rich, so free;
Say, while lost in holy wonder,—
Why, O Lord, such love to me?
Hallelujah!
Grace shall reign eternally.

206   8, 7.

" The Lord Jehovah is my strength and my song ; he also is become my salvation."

1. CALL Jehovah thy salvation,
Rest beneath th' Almighty's shade,
In His secret habitation
Dwell, nor ever be dismayed!

2. There no tumult can alarm thee,
Thou shalt dread no hidden snare;

Guile nor violence can harm thee,
In eternal safeguard there.

3. Thee, though winds and waves are swelling,
God, thy hope, shall bear through all;
Plague shall not come nigh thy dwelling,
Thee no evil shall befall.

4. He shall charge his angel legions
Watch and ward o'er thee to keep;
Though thou walk through hostile regions,
Though in desert wilds thou sleep.

5. Since, with firm and pure affection,
Thou on God hast set thy love,
With the wings of His protection
He shall shield thee from above.

207
8, 7.

*"These . . . confessed that they were
strangers and pilgrims on the earth."*

1. RISE, my soul, thy God directs thee,
Stranger hands no more impede;
Pass thou on, His strength protects thee,
Strength that has the captive freed.

2. Light divine surrounds thy going,
God Himself shall mark the way;
Secret blessings, richly flowing,
Lead to everlasting day.

3. Though thy way be long and dreary,
Eagle strength He'll still renew;
Garments fresh, and feet unweary,
Tell how God will bear thee through:

179

4. Till to Canaan's long-loved dwelling
    Love divine thy foot shall bring,
There, with shouts of triumph swelling,
    Zion's songs in rest to sing.

208   **7, 6.**

"And, having done all, to stand."

1. STAND up ! stand up for Jesus !
      Ye soldiers of the cross ;
    Lift high His royal banner,
      It must not suffer loss ;
    From victory unto victory
      His army He shall lead,
    Till every foe is vanquished,
      And Christ is Lord indeed.

2. Stand up ! stand up for Jesus !
      The trumpet call obey ;
    Forth to the mighty conflict,
      In this His glorious day :
    ' Ye that are men, now serve Him,'
      Against unnumbered foes ;
    Your courage rise with danger,
      And strength to strength oppose.

3. Stand up ! stand up for Jesus !
      Stand in His strength alone ;
    The arm of flesh will fail you —
      Ye dare not trust your own :
    Put on the gospel armour,
      And, watching unto prayer,
    Where duty calls or danger,
      Be never wanting there !

4. Stand up ! stand up for Jesus !
      The strife will not be long ;

This day the noise of battle,
  The next the victor's song:
To him that overcometh,
  A crown of life shall be:
He with the King of Glory
  Shall reign eternally.

209   S. M.

" Put on the whole armour of God."

1. SOLDIERS of Christ, arise,
     And put your armour on,
  Strong in the strength which God supplies
     Through His eternal Son: ·

2. Strong in the Lord of Hosts,
     And in His mighty power;
  Who in the strength of Jesus trusts
     Is more than conqueror. ·

3. Stand, then, in His great might,
     With all His strength endued;
  But take, to arm you for the fight,
     The panoply of God.

4. From strength to strength go on,
     Wrestle and fight and pray,
  Tread all the powers of darkness down,
     And win the well-fought day;

5. That, having all things done,
     And all your conflicts past,
  You may o'ercome through Christ alone
     And stand complete at last.

**IMAGE EVALUATION
TEST TARGET (MT-3)**

6"

Photographic
Sciences
Corporation

23 WEST MAIN STREET
WEBSTER, N.Y. 14580
(716) 872-4503

210

7s.

"Fight the good fight of faith."

1. MUCH in sorrow, oft in woe,
   Onward, Christians, onward go;
   Fight the fight, maintain the strife,
   Strengthened with the bread of life!

2. Onward, Christians, onward go;
   Join the war, and face the foe;
   Faint not! much doth yet remain,
   Dreary is the long campaign.

3. Shrink not, Christians; will ye yield?
   Will ye quit the painful field?
   Will ye flee in danger's hour?
   Know ye not your Captain's power?

4. Let your drooping hearts be glad;
   March in heavenly armour clad:
   Fight, nor think the battle long,
   Victory soon shall tune your song.

5. Let not sorrow dim your eye,
   Soon shall every tear be dry;
   Let not woe your course impede,
   Great your strength, if great your need.

6. Onward then to battle move,
   More than conquerors ye shall prove:
   Though opposed by many a foe,
   Christian soldiers, onward go!

211   S. M.

*" O taste and see that the Lord is good ;
blessed is the man that trusteth in
him."*

1. Your harps, ye trembling saints,
   Down from the willows take ;
Loud, to the praise of love divine,
   Bid every string awake.

2. Though in a foreign land,
   We are not far from home,
And nearer to our house above
   We every moment come.

3. His grace will to the end
   Stronger and brighter shine ;
Nor present things, nor things to come,
   Shall quench the spark divine.

4. When we in darkness walk,
   Nor feel the heavenly flame,
Then is the time to trust our God,
   And rest upon His name.

5. Soon shall our doubts and fears
   Subside at His control;
His loving kindness shall break through
   The midnight of the soul.

6. Blest is the man, O God,
   That stays himself on Thee!
Who wait for Thy salvation, Lord,
   Shall Thy salvation see.

212

8, 7.

" I will hear what God the Lord will speak."

1. HEAR what God the Lord hath spoken:
   'O my people, faint and few,
   Comfortless, afflicted, broken,
   Fair abodes I build for you.

2. 'Thorns of heartfelt tribulation
   Shall no more perplex your ways;
   You shall name your walls Salvation,
   And your gates shall all be Praise.

3. 'There, in undisturbed possession,
   Peace and righteousness shall reign;
   Never shall you feel oppression,
   Hear no voice of war again.

4. 'God shall rise, and shining o'er you,
   Change to day the gloom of night;
   He, the Lord, shall be your Glory,
   God, your everlasting Light.'

213

6, 5.

" In the name of our God we will set up our banners."

1. BRIGHTLY gleams our banner
   Pointing to the sky,
   Waving wanderers onward
   To their home on high.
   Journeying o'er the desert,
   Gladly thus we pray,
   And with hearts united
   Take our heavenward way.

Brightly gleams our banner
Pointing to the sky,
Waving wanderers onward
To their home on high.

2. Jesus, Lord and Master,
At Thy sacred feet,
Here with hearts rejoicing
See Thy children meet;
Often have we left Thee,
Often gone astray,
Keep us, mighty Saviour,
In the narrow way.
Brightly gleams, &c.

3. All our days direct us
In the way we go,
Lead us on victorious
Over every foe:
Bid Thine angels shield us
When the storm-clouds lower,
Pardon, Lord, and save us
In the last dread hour.
Brightly gleams, &c.

214 7s.

" Lovest thou me ?"

1. HARK, my soul, it is the Lord;
'Tis thy Saviour, hear His word;
Jesus speaks, and speaks to thee:
' Say, poor sinner, lov'st thou Me?

2. ' I delivered thee when bound,
And, when bleeding, healed thy wound;
Sought thee wandering, set thee right,
Turned thy darkness into light.

3. 'Can a woman's tender care
   Cease toward the child she bare?
   Yes, she may forgetful be,
   Yet will I remember thee.

4. 'Mine is an unchanging love,
   Higher than the heights above;
   Deeper than the depths beneath,
   Free and faithful, strong as death.

5. 'Thou shalt see My glory soon,
   When the work of grace is done;
   Partner of My throne shalt be:
   Say, poor sinner, lov'st thou Me?'

6. Lord, it is my chief complaint
   That my love is cold and faint;
   Yet I love Thee and adore,
   O for grace to love Thee more!

215

II S.

*'This is the name whereby he shall be
called, The Lord Our Righteousness.'*

1. I ONCE was a stranger to grace and to God,
   I knew not my danger, and felt not my load;
   Though friends spoke in rapture of Christ on
   the tree,
   'Jehovah Tsidkenu;' 'twas nothing to me.

2. Like tears from the daughters of Zion that roll,
   I wept when the waters went over his soul;
   Yet thought not that my sins had nailed to the
   tree
   'Jehovah Tsidkenu;' 'twas nothing to me.

3. When free grace awoke me, by light from on
    high,
   Then legal fears shook me, I trembled to die;
   No refuge, no safety in self could I see —
   'Jehovah Tsidkenu' my Saviour must be.

4. My terrors all vanished before the sweet name;
   My guilty fears banished, with boldness I came
   To drink at the fountain, life-giving and free;
   'Jehovah Tsidkenu' is all things to me.

5. Even treading the valley, the shadow of death,
   This watchword shall rally my faltering breath;
   For if from life's fever my God set me free,
   'Jehovah Tsidkenu' my death song shall be.

6. Jehovah Tsidkenu! my treasure and boast,
   Jehovah Tsidkenu! I ne'er can be lost;
   In Thee I shall conquer by flood and by field,
   My cable, my anchor, my breastplate and shield!

216   P. M.

"Be of good cheer; it is I."

1. O THOU that on the billow
        Couldest sleep
   While tempests round Thy pillow
        Fierce did sweep —
   Grant us Thy holy peace,
   While the tumults rage around us,
   And the perils still increase,
        Our hearts to keep.

2. O Thou that in the night storm
        Drewest nigh,
   Appearing as a bright form
        From on high —

Still 'mid our gloom appear;
Guide us gently to our haven;
Give our fainting spirits cheer,
 Say 'Lo, 'tis I!'

3. O Thou that stood'st at morning
  On the shore,
To bless the bark returning,
  And the store —
Bid us such welcome blest,
When, beyond those troubled waters,
From our night-long toil we rest
  For evermore.

217   8s.

*" In that he himself hath suffered, be-
ing tempted, he is able to succour
them that are tempted."*

1. WHEN gathering clouds around I view,
And days are dark, and friends are few,
On Him I lean, who not in vain
Experienced every human pain;
He sees my wants, allays my fears,
And counts and treasures up my tears.

2. If aught should tempt my soul to stray
From heavenly wisdom's narrow way,
To fly the good I would pursue,
Or do the sin I would not do,
Still He, who felt temptation's power,
Shall guard me in that dangerous hour.

3. If vexing thoughts within me rise,
And sore dismayed my spirit dies;
Still He, who once vouchsafed to bear
The sickening anguish of despair,
Shall sweetly soothe, shall gently dry,
The throbbing heart, the streaming eye.

4. When sorrowing o'er some stone I bend,
Which covers what was once a friend,
And from his voice, his hand, his smile,
Divides me for a little while;
Thou, Saviour, mark'st the tears I shed,
For Thou didst weep o'er Lazarus dead.

5. And O, when I have safely passed
Through every conflict but the last,
Still, still unchanging, watch beside
My painful bed, for Thou hast died;
Then point to realms of cloudless day,
And wipe the latest tear away.

218   C. M.

"We . . . have fled for refuge to lay
hold upon the hope set before us."

1. DEAR refuge of my weary soul,
   On Thee, when sorrows rise,
   On Thee, when waves of trouble roll,
   My fainting hope relies.

2. To Thee I tell each rising grief,
   For Thou alone canst heal;
   Thy word can bring a sweet relief
   For every pain I feel.

3. But oh! when gloomy doubts prevail,
   I fear to call Thee mine:
   The springs of comfort seem to fail,
   And all my hopes decline.

4. Yet, gracious God, where shall I flee?
   Thou art my only trust;
   And still my soul will cleave to Thee,
   Though prostrate in the dust.

5. Thy mercy-seat is open still,
   Here let my soul retreat;
With humble hope attend Thy will,
   And wait beneath Thy feet.

219   8, 7.

" As seeing him who is invisible."

1. ALL unseen the Master walketh
      By the toiling servant's side;
   Comfortable words He speaketh,
      While His hands uphold and guide.

2. Grief, nor pain, nor any sorrow
      Rends thy heart, to Him unknown;
   He to-day and He to-morrow,
      Grace sufficient gives His own.

3. Holy strivings nerve and strengthen,
      Long endurance wins the crown:
   When the evening shadows lengthen,
      Thou shalt lay thy burden down.

220   S. M.

*" Watch, therefore, for ye know not what
    hour your Lord doth come."*

1. YE servants of the Lord,
      Each in his office wait,
   Observant of His heavenly word,
      And watchful at His gate.

2. Let all your lamps be bright,
      And trim the golden flame;
   Gird up your loins, as in His sight,
      For awful is His name.

3. Watch! 'tis your Lord's command,
      And while we speak He's near;

Mark the first signal of His hand,
And ready all appear.

4. O happy servant he,
In such a posture found!
He shall his Lord with rapture see,
And be with honour crowned.

221   7, 3.

*" Watch and pray, that ye enter not into
temptation."*

1. CHRISTIAN! seek not yet repose,
Cast thy dreams of ease away;
Thou art in the midst of foes;
'Watch and pray.'

2. Principalities and powers,
Mustering their unseen array,
Wait for thy unguarded hours;
'Watch and pray.'

3. Gird thy heavenly armour on,
Wear it ever night and day;
Ambushed lies the evil one;
'Watch and pray.'

4. Watch, as if on that alone
Hung the issue of the day;
Pray, that help may be sent down;
'Watch and pray.'

222   7, 6.

" The Lord is my light, and my salvation."

1. GOD is my strong salvation,
What foe have I to fear?
In darkness and temptation,
My light, my help, is near.

2. Though hosts encamp around me,
    Firm to the fight I stand:
What terror can confound me,
    With God at my right hand?

3. Place on the Lord reliance:
    My soul, with courage wait;
His truth be thine affiance,
    When faint and desolate.

4. His might thy heart shall strengthen,
    His love thy joy increase;
Mercy thy days shall lengthen;
    The Lord will give thee peace.

223   11s.

" The Lord your God, which goeth before
you, he shall fight for you."

1. ONWARD, Christian soldiers, marching as to
        war,
    Looking unto Jesus who is gone before,
    Christ, the Royal Master, leads against the
        foe,
    Forward into battle, see His banners go.

        Onward, Christian soldiers, marching as to
            war,
        Looking unto Jesus who is gone before.

2. At the name of Jesus, Satan's host doth flee;
    On, then, Christian soldiers, on to victory!
    Hell's foundations quiver at the shout of
        praise:
    Brothers, lift your voices; loud your anthems
        raise.
                Onward, Christian soldiers, &c.

3. Like a mighty army, moves the Church of God.
Brothers, we are treading where the saints have
trod.
We are not divided, all one body we —
One in hope and doctrine, one in charity.
Onward, Christian soldiers, &c.

4. Crowns and thrones may perish, kingdoms rise
and wane;
But the Church of Jesus constant will remain:
Gates of hell can never 'gainst that Church pre-
vail:
We have Christ's own promise, that can never
fail.
Onward, Christian soldiers, &c.

5. Onward, then, ye people, join our happy throng;
Blend with ours your voices in the triumph-
song;
Glory, praise, and honour unto Christ the King,
This through countless ages men and angels
sing.
Onward, Christian soldiers, &c.

224   7s.

*" The ransomed of the Lord shall return,
and come to Zion with songs."*

1. CHILDREN of the heavenly King,
As ye journey sweetly sing:
Sing your Saviour's worthy praise,
Glorious in His works and ways.

2. We are travelling home to God,
In the way the fathers trod:
They are happy now, and we
Soon their happiness shall see.

3. Shout, ye little flock and blest;
   You on Jesus' throne shall rest:
   There your seat is now prepared,
   There your kingdom and reward.

4. Lift your eyes, ye sons of light,
   Zion's city is in sight:
   There our endless home shall be,
   There our Lord we soon shall see.

5. Fear not, brethren; joyful stand
   On the borders of your land;
   Jesus Christ, your Father's Son,
   Bids you undismayed go on.

6. Lord, obediently we go,
   Gladly leaving all below,
   Only Thou our leader be
   And we still will follow Thee.

225　　　　　　　　　　　　S. M.

*" Let the children of Zion be joyful in
their King."*

1. COME, ye that love the Lord,
   And let your joys be known;
   Join in a song with sweet accord,
   And thus surround the throne.

2. Let those refuse to sing
   That never knew our God;
   But children of the heavenly King
   May speak their joys abroad.

3. The men of grace have found
   Glory begun below;
   Celestial fruits on earthly ground
   From faith and hope may grow.

4. The hill of Zion yields
 A thousand sacred sweets,
Before we reach the heavenly fields,
 Or walk the golden streets.

5. Then let our songs abound,
 And every tear be dry;
We're marching through Immanuel's ground,
 To fairer worlds on high.

226
7, 6.

*." Weeping may endure for a night, but
joy cometh in the morning."*

1. SOMETIMES a light surprises
 The Christian while he sings;
It is the Lord who rises
 With healing in His wings:
When comforts are declining,
 He grants the soul again
A season of clear shining,
 To cheer it after rain.

2. In holy contemplation,
 We sweetly then pursue
The theme of God's salvation,
 And find it ever new:
Set free from present sorrow,
 We cheerfully can say,
Even let the unknown to-morrow
 Bring with it what it may;

3. It can bring with it nothing,
 But He will bear us through;
Who gives the lilies clothing,
 Will clothe His people too

Beneath the spreading heavens,
No creature but is fed;
And He who feeds the ravens,
Will give His children bread.

4. Though vine nor fig-tree neither,
Their wonted fruit shall bear,
Though all the field should wither,
Nor flocks nor herds be there;
Yet, God the same abiding,
His praise shall tune my voice;
For while in Him confiding,
I cannot but rejoice.

227   8, 7, 6.

" God is our refuge and strength."

1. A SAFE stronghold our God is still,
A trusty shield and weapon;
By His right arm He surely will
Free from all ills that happen.
For still our ancient foe
Doth seek to work us woe;
Strong mail of craft and power
He weareth in this hour;
On earth is not his fellow.

2. Stood we alone in our own might,
Our striving would be losing;
For us the one true Man doth fight,
The Man of God's own choosing.
Who is this chosen One?
'Tis Jesus Christ, the Son,
The Lord of hosts, 'tis He
Who wins the victory
In every field of battle.

3. And were the world with devils filled,
   And watching to devour us,
Our souls to fear we need not yield,
   They cannot overpower us ;
      Their dreaded Prince no more
      Can harm us as of yore;
      His rage we can endure ;
      For lo! his doom is sure,
A word shall overthrow him.

4. Still must they leave God's word its might,
   For which no thanks they merit;
Still is He with us in the fight,
   With His good gifts and Spirit.
      Even should they, in the strife,
      Take kindred, goods, and life,
      We freely let them go,
      They profit not the foe ;
With us remains the kingdom.

228   7, 6.

" Endeavouring to keep the unity of the
Spirit in the bond of peace."

1. OUR blessed bond of union,
   Thou art, O Christ, our Lord !
The rule of our communion
   Is thine own faithful word.
Thou art our Elder Brother,
   Who, to redeem us, died :
To Thee, and to none other,
   Our souls we do confide.

2. Thy peace in us abounding,
   Thy presence ever sure,
Thy light our path surrounding,
   Thy strength to us secure.

Beneath Thy banner glorious,
    Clad in Thine armour true,
We shall march on victorious,
    And all our foes subdue.

3. Saviour, most true and gracious,
    Thy Spirit now impart,
And let Thy love most precious
    Possess and fill each heart.
We grasp Thy promise given,
    We set before our eyes
One faith, one hope, one heaven,
    One battle, and one prize.

229   8s.

*" The Lord is my rock and my fortress,
and my deliverer, my God, my strength,
in whom I will trust."*

1. WHY should I fear the darkest hour,
    Or tremble at the tempter's power?
    Jesus vouchsafes to be my tower.

2. Though hot the fight, why quit the field?
    Why must I either flee or yield,
    Since Jesus is my mighty shield?

3. When creature-comforts fade and die,
    Worldlings may weep, but why should I?
    Jesus still lives, and still is nigh.

4. Though all the flocks and herds were dead,
    My soul a famine need not dread,
    For Jesus is my living bread.

5. I know not what may soon betide,
    Or how my wants shall be supplied;
    But Jesus knows, and will provide.

6. Though sin would fill me with distress,
The throne of grace I dare address,
For Jesus is my righteousness.

7. Though faint my prayers, and cold my love,
My steadfast hope shall not remove,
While Jesus intercedes above.

8. Against me earth and hell combine;
But on my side is power divine;
Jesus is all, and He is mine.

230   S. M.

" By grace ye are saved."

1. GRACE ! 'tis a charming sound,
Harmonious to my ear;
Heaven with the echo shall resound,
And all the earth shall hear.

2. Grace first contrived a way
To save rebellious man ;
And all the steps that grace display
Which drew the wondrous plan.

3. Grace taught my wandering feet
To tread the heavenly road ;
And new supplies each hour I meet,
While pressing on to God.

4. Grace all the work shall crown,
Through everlasting days ;
It lays in heaven the topmost stone,
And well deserves the praise.

V. — *THE CHURCH.*

231   8, 7.

" Glorious things are spoken of thee,
O city of God."

1. GLORIOUS things of thee are spoken,
   Zion, city of our God;
   He, whose word cannot be broken,
   Formed thee for His own abode.

2. On the Rock of Ages founded,
   What can shake thy sure repose?
   With salvation's walls surrounded,
   Thou may'st smile at all thy foes.

3. See, the streams of living waters,
   Springing from eternal love,
   Well supply thy sons and daughters,
   And all fear of want remove.

4. Who can faint while such a river
   Ever flows their thirst t' assuage, —
   Grace which, like the Lord the giver,
   Never fails from age to age?

5. Saviour, if of Zion's city
   I through grace a member am;
   Let the world deride or pity,
   I will glory in Thy name:

6. Fading is the worldling's pleasure,
   All his boasted pomp and show:
Solid joys and lasting treasure,
   None but Zion's children know.

232

S. M.

" If I forget thee, O Jerusalem, let my
right hand forget her cunning."

1. I LOVE Thy kingdom, Lord,
   The house of Thine abode,
The Church, our blest Redeemer saved
   With his own precious blood.

2. I love Thy Church, O God!
   Her walls before Thee stand,
Dear as the apple of Thine eye,
   And graven on Thy hand.

3. For her my tears shall fall,
   For her my prayers ascend;
To her my cares and toils be given,
   Till toils and cares shall end.

4. Beyond my highest joy
   I prize her heavenly ways,
Her sweet communion, solemn vows,
   Her hymns of love and praise.

5. Jesus, Thou Friend divine,
   Our Saviour, and our King!
Thy hand from every snare and foe,
   Shall great deliverance bring.

6. Sure as Thy truth shall last,
   To Zion shall be given
The brightest glories earth can yield,
   And brighter bliss of heaven.

233

7, 6.

" Other foundation can no man lay."

1. THE Church's one foundation
      Is Jesus Christ, her Lord;
   She is His new creation
      By water and the Word:
   From heaven He came and sought her,
      To be His holy bride;
   With His own blood He bought her,
      And for her life He died.

2. Elect from every nation,
      Yet one o'er all the earth,
   Her charter of salvation
      One Lord, one faith, one birth,
   One holy name she blesses,
      Partakes one holy food,
   And to one hope she presses
      With every grace endued.

3. Though with a scornful wonder
      Men see her sore opprest,
   By schisms rent asunder,
      By heresies distrest,
   Yet saints their watch are keeping,
      Their cry goes up, ' How long?'
   And soon the night of weeping
      Shall be the morn of song.

4. 'Mid toil, and tribulation,
      And tumult of her war,
   She waits the consummation
      Of peace for evermore;
   Till with the vision glorious
      Her longing eyes are blest,
   And the great Church victorious
      Shall be the Church at rest.

5. Yet she on earth hath union
    With God the Three in One,
And mystic sweet communion
    With those whose rest is won:
O happy ones and holy!
    Lord, give us grace that we,
Like them the meek and lowly,
    On high may dwell with Thee.

234   **8, 7.**

*" Behold, I lay in Zion for a foundation
a stone, a tried stone, a precious
corner-stone, a sure foundation."*

1. CHRIST is made the sure foundation,
    Christ the head and corner-stone,
Chosen of the Lord, and precious,
    Binding all the Church in one,
Holy Zion's help for ever,
    And her confidence alone.

2. To this temple, where we call Thee,
    Come, O Lord of hosts, to-day;
With Thy wonted loving-kindness,
    Hear Thy servants, as they pray;
And Thy fullest benediction
    Shed within its walls alway.

3. Here vouchsafe to all Thy servants
    What they ask of Thee to gain,
What they gain from Thee for ever
    With the blessèd to retain,
And hereafter in Thy glory
    Evermore with Thee to reign.

4. Praise and honour to the Father,
    Praise and honour to the Son,
Praise and honour to the Spirit,
    Ever Three, and ever One,
One in might, and One in glory,
    While eternal ages run.

235   **6, 4.**

*"Jesus Christ himself being the chief
corner-stone."*

1. CHRIST is our corner-stone,
   On Him alone we build;
   With His true saints alone
   The courts of heaven are filled:
   On His great love
   Our hopes we place
   Of present grace
   And joys above.

2. O then with hymns of praise
   These hallowed courts shall ring;
   Our voices we will raise
   The Three in One to sing;
   And thus proclaim
   In joyful song,
   Both loud and long,
   That glorious name.

3. Here, gracious God, do Thou
   For evermore draw nigh;
   Accept each faithful vow,
   And mark each suppliant sigh:
   In copious shower
   On all who pray,
   Each holy day,
   Thy blessing pour.

4. Here may we gain from heaven
   The grace which we implore;
   And may that grace, once given,
   Be with us evermore,
   Until that day
   When all the blest
   To endless rest
   Are called away!

236

L. M.

" The sabbath a delight."

1. ANOTHER six days' work is done,
   Another Sabbath is begun:
   Return, my soul; enjoy thy rest;
   Improve the day thy God hath blessed.

2. O that our thoughts and thanks may rise
   As grateful incense to the skies;
   And draw from heaven that sweet repose
   Which none, but he that feels it, knows.

3. This heavenly calm within the breast
   Is the sure pledge of glorious rest,
   Which for the Church of God remains,
   The end of cares, the end of pains.

4. In holy duties let the day,
   In holy pleasures, pass away:
   How sweet a Sabbath thus to spend
   In hope of one that ne'er shall end!

237

7s.

*" Ye shall keep my sabbaths and rever-
ence my sanctuary."*

1. SAFELY through another week,
   God hath brought us on our way;
   Let us now a blessing seek,
   Waiting in His courts to-day:
   Day of all the week the best,
   Emblem of eternal rest.

2. While we seek supplies of grace,
   Through the dear Redeemer's name,
   Show Thy reconciling face,
   Take away our sin and shame;

From our worldly cares set free,
May we rest this day in Thee.

3. Here we come Thy name to praise;
    Let us feel Thy presence near;
May Thy glory meet our eyes,
    While we in Thy house appear:
Here afford us, Lord, a taste
Of our everlasting rest.

4. May the gospel's joyful sound
    Wake our minds to raptures new;
Let Thy victories abound,
    Unrepenting souls subdue:
Thus let all our Sabbaths prove,
Till we rest in Thee above.

238   6, 8.

*" This is the day which the Lord hath
made ; we will rejoice and be glad
in it."*

1. AWAKE, ye saints, awake,
    And hail the sacred day;
In loftiest songs of praise
    Your joyful homage pay:
Come bless the day that God hath blest,
The type of heaven's eternal rest.

2. On this auspicious morn
    The Lord of life arose;
He burst the bars of death,
    And vanquished all our foes;
And now He pleads our cause above,
And reaps the fruit of all His love.

3. All hail! triumphant Lord,
    Heaven with hosannas rings;

And earth, in humbler strains,
　Thy praise responsive sings:
Worthy the Lamb, that once was slain,
Through endless years to live and reign.

4. Great King, gird on Thy sword,
　Ascend Thy conquering car,
While justice, power, and love
　Maintain the glorious war:
This day let sinners own Thy sway,
And rebels cast their arms away.

239 S. M.

" I was in the Spirit on the Lord's day."

1. THIS is the day of light:
　Let there be light to-day;
O Dayspring, rise upon our night,
　And chase its gloom away.

2. This is the day of rest:
　Our failing strength renew;
On weary brain and troubled breast
　Shed Thou Thy freshening dew.

3. This is the day of peace:
　Thy peace our spirits fill:
Bid Thou the blasts of discord cease,
　The waves of strife be still.

4. This is the day of prayer:
　Let earth to heaven draw near;
Lift up our hearts to seek Thee there,
　Come down to meet us here.

5. This is the first of days:
　Send forth Thy quickening breath,
And wake dead souls to love and praise,
　O Vanquisher of death!

240 7s.

"I gave them my sabbaths, to be a sign between me and them."

1. HAIL, thou bright and sacred morn,
   Risen with gladness in thy beams!
Light, which not of earth is born,
   From thy dawn in glory streams:
Airs of heaven are breathed around,
And each place is holy ground.

2. Great Creator! who this day
   From Thy perfect work didst rest;
By the souls that own Thy sway,
   Hallowed be its hours and blest:
Cares of earth aside be thrown,
This day given to heaven alone!

3. Saviour, who this day didst break
   The dark prison of the tomb,
Bid my slumbering soul awake,
   Shine through all its sin and gloom;
Let me, from my bonds set free,
Rise from sin and live to Thee.

4. Blessèd Spirit, Comforter,
   Sent this day from Christ on high;
Lord, on me Thy gifts confer,
   Cleanse, illumine, sanctify!
All Thine influence shed abroad;
Lead me to the truth of God.

241 7, 6.

" This is the rest wherewith ye may cause the weary to rest."

1 O DAY of rest and gladness,
   O day of joy and light,
O balm of care and sadness,
   Most beautiful, most bright!

On thee the high and lowly,
  Before the eternal Throne,
Sing Holy, Holy, Holy,
  To the great Three in One.

2. On thee, at the creation,
    The light first had its birth ;
  On thee for our salvation
    Christ rose from depths of earth ;
  On thee our Lord victorious
    The Spirit sent from heaven ;
  And thus on thee most glorious
    A triple light was given.

3. Thou art a cooling fountain
    In life's dry dreary sand ;
  From thee, like Pisgah's mountain
    We view our promised land ;
  A day of sweet refection,
    A day of holy love,
  A day of resurrection
    From earth to things above.

4. To-day on weary nations
    The heavenly manna falls ;
  To holy convocations
    The silver trumpet calls,
  Where Gospel light is glowing
    With pure and radiant beams,
  And living water flowing
    With soul-refreshing streams.

5. New graces ever gaining
    From this our day of rest,
  We reach the rest remaining
    To spirits of the blest.
  To Holy Ghost be praises,
    To Father, and to Son ;
  The Church her voice upraises
    To Thee, blest Three in One.

242 L. M.

*" There remaineth, therefore, a rest to
the people of God."*

1. LORD of the Sabbath! hear us pray,
   In this Thy house, on this Thy day;
   And own as grateful sacrifice
   The songs which from Thy people rise.

2. Thine earthly Sabbaths, Lord, we love;
   But there's a nobler rest above;
   To that our labouring souls aspire
   With ardent hope and strong desire.

3. No more fatigue, no more distress;
   No guilt the conscience to oppress;
   No groans to mingle with the songs
   Resounding from immortal tongues:

4. No rude alarms of raging foes;
   No cares to break the long repose,
   No midnight shade, no clouded sun,
   But sacred, high, eternal noon.

5. O long-expected day, begin!
   Dawn on these realms of woe and sin!
   Fain would we leave this weary road,
   And sleep in death, to rest with God!

243 L. M.

*" It is a good thing to give thanks unto
the Lord."*

1. SWEET is the work, my God, my King,
   To praise Thy name, give thanks and sing;
   To show Thy love by morning light,
   And talk of all Thy truth at night.

2. Sweet is the day of sacred rest,
   No mortal cares shall seize my breast;
   O may my heart in tune be found,
   Like David's harp of solemn sound.

3. My heart shall triumph in my Lord,
   And bless His works, and bless His word:
   Thy works of grace, how bright they shine!
   How deep Thy counsels! how divine!

4. Then shall I share a glorious part,
   When grace hath well refined my heart,
   And fresh supplies of joy are shed,
   Like holy oil to cheer my head.

5. Then shall I see and hear and know
   All I desired or wished below;
   And every power find sweet employ
   In that eternal world of joy.

244   L. M.

*" Lord, I have loved the habitation of thy
house, and the place where thine
honour dwelleth."*

1. SWEET is the solemn voice that calls
      The Christian to the house of prayer;
   I love to stand within its walls,
      For Thou, O Lord, art present there.

2. I love to tread the hallowed courts,
      Where two or three for worship meet;
   For thither Christ Himself resorts,
      And makes the little band complete.

3. 'Tis sweet to raise the common song,
      To join in holy praise and love,
   And imitate the blessèd throng
      That mingle hearts and songs above.

4. Within these walls may peace abound ;
   May all our hearts in one agree !
Where brethren meet, where Christ is found,
   May peace and concord ever be !

245   7s.

*" For a day in thy courts is better than
a thousand."*

1. PLEASANT are Thy courts above,
   In the land of light and love ;
   Pleasant are Thy courts below,
   In this land of sin and woe.
   O, my spirit longs and faints
   For the converse of Thy saints,
   For the brightness of Thy face,
   For Thy fulness, God of grace.

2. Happy birds that sing and fly
   Round Thy altars, O Most High
   Happier souls that find a rest
   In a heavenly Father's breast !
   Like the wandering dove, that found
   No repose on earth around,
   They can to their ark repair,
   And enjoy it ever there.

3. Happy souls ! their praises flow
   Even in this vale of woe ;
   Waters in the desert rise,
   Manna feeds them from the skies ;
   On they go from strength to strength,
   Till they reach Thy throne at length,
   At Thy feet adoring fall,
   Who hast led them safe through all.

4. Lord, be mine this prize to win ;
   Guide me through a world of sin :

Keep me by Thy saving grace;
Give me at Thy side a place:
Sun and shield alike Thou art;
Guide and guard my erring heart.
Grace and glory flow from Thee;
Shower, O shower them, Lord, on me!

246   6, 4.

*"How amiable are thy tabernacles,
Lord God of hosts!"*

1. LORD of the worlds above,
      How pleasant and how fair
   The dwellings of Thy love,
      Thy earthly temples, are!
         To Thine abode
            My heart aspires,
            With warm desires,
         To see my God.

2. O happy souls that pray
      Where God appoints to hear!
   O happy men that pay
      Their constant service there!
         They praise Thee still;
            And happy they
            That love the way
         To Zion's hill.

3. They go from strength to strength
      Through this dark vale of tears,
   Till each arrives at length,
      Till each in heaven appears:
         O glorious seat,
            When God our King
            Shall thither bring
         Our willing feet!

247
8s.

" Surely the Lord is in this place."

1. Lo! God is here! let us adore,
    And own how dreadful is this place!
Let all within us feel His power,
    And silent bow before His face;
Who know His power, His grace who prove,
Serve Him with awe, with reverence love.

2. Lo! God is here! Him day and night
    The united choirs of angels sing;
To Him enthroned above all height,
    Heaven's hosts their noblest praises bring:
Disdain not, Lord, our meaner song,
Who praise Thee with a stammering tongue.

3. Gladly the toys of earth we leave,
    Wealth, pleasure, fame, for Thee alone;
To Thee our will, soul, flesh, we give,
    O take, O seal them for Thine own!
Thou art the God! Thou art the Lord!
Be Thou by all Thy works adored.

4. Being of beings! may our praise
    Thy courts with grateful fragrance fill;
Still may we stand before Thy face,
    Still hear and do Thy sovereign will;
To Thee may all our thoughts arise,
Ceaseless, accepted sacrifice.

248
L. M.

*" Where two or three are gathered to-
gether in my name, there am I in
the midst of them."*

1. JESUS, where'er Thy people meet,
    There they behold Thy mercy-seat;
Where'er they seek Thee Thou art found,
And every place is hallowed ground.

2. For Thou, within no walls confined,
   Inhabitest the humble mind;
   Such ever bring Thee where they come,
   And going, take Thee to their home.

3. Dear Shepherd of Thy chosen few,
   Thy former mercies here renew;
   Here to our waiting hearts proclaim
   The sweetness of Thy saving name.

4. Here may we prove the power of prayer
   To strengthen faith and sweeten care,
   To teach our faint desires to rise,
   And bring all heaven before our eyes.

5. Lord, we are few, but Thou art near;
   Nor short Thine arm, nor deaf Thine ear;
   O rend the heavens, come quickly down,
   And make a thousand hearts Thine own!

249   L. M.

*" There the Lord commanded the blessing,
even life for evermore."*

1. COMMAND Thy blessing from above,
   O God, on all assembled here;
   Behold us with a Father's love,
   While we look up with filial fear.

2. Command Thy blessing, Jesus, Lord;
   May we Thy true disciples be;
   Speak to each heart the mighty word,
   Say to the weakest, 'Follow me.'

3. Command Thy blessing in this hour,
   Spirit of truth, and fill the place
   With humbling and exalting power,
   With quickening and confirming grace.

4. O Thou, our Maker, Saviour, Guide,
    One true eternal God confessed!
Whom Thou hast joined may none divide,
    None dare to curse whom Thou hast blessed.

5. With Thee and these for ever found,
    May all the souls who here unite,
With harps and songs Thy throne surround,
    Rest in Thy love and reign in light.

250   L. M.

" They watch for your souls as they that
must give account."

1. LORD, pour Thy Spirit from on high,
    And Thine ordainèd servants bless;
Graces and gifts to each supply,
    And clothe Thy priests with righteousness.

2. Within Thy temple, when they stand
    To teach the truth, as taught by Thee,
Saviour, like stars in Thy right hand
    Let all Thy Church's pastors be.

3. Wisdom, and zeal, and love impart,
    Firmness with meekness from above,
To bear Thy people in their heart,
    And love the souls whom Thou dost love:

4. To love, and pray, and never faint,
    By day and night their guard to keep,
To warn the sinner, form the saint,
    To feed Thy lambs, and tend Thy sheep.

5. So when their work is finished here,
    They may in hope their charge resign;
When the chief Shepherd shall appear,
    They may with crowns of glory shine!

251 S. M.

*" How beautiful upon the mountains are
the feet of him that bringeth good
tidings!"*

1. How beauteous are their feet
   Who stand on Zion's hill,
Who bring salvation on their tongues,
   And words of peace reveal!

2. How charming is their voice,
   How sweet the tidings are!
Zion, behold thy Saviour King;
   He reigns and triumphs here.

3. How happy are our ears
   That hear this joyful sound,
Which kings and prophets waited for,
   And sought, but never found!

4. How blessèd are our eyes
   That see this heavenly light!
Prophets and kings desired it long,
   But died without the sight.

5. The watchmen join their voice,
   And tuneful notes employ;
Jerusalem breaks forth in songs,
   And deserts learn the joy.

6. The Lord makes bare His arm,
   Through all the earth abroad;
Let every nation now behold
   Their Saviour and their God.

252   S. M.

"Keep the unity of the Spirit in the bond
of peace."

1. BLEST be the tie that binds
    Our hearts in Christian love;
  The fellowship of kindred minds
    Is like to that above.

2. Before our Father's throne
    We pour our ardent prayers:
  Our fears, our hopes, our aims are one,
    Our comforts and our cares.

3. We share our mutual woes,
    Our mutual burdens bear;
  And often for each other flows
    The sympathising tear.

4. But glorious hope revives
    Our courage by the way;
  While each in expectation lives,
    And longs to see the day.

5. From sorrow, toil, and pain,
    And sin we shall be free;
  And perfect love and friendship reign
    Through all eternity.

253   7s.

"Jesus sat over against the treasury,
and beheld how the people cast
money into the treasury."

1. JESUS, Lord, we humbly pray,
  Take our gifts on this Thy day:
  Gladly, gratefully we give,
  Of Thy grace do Thou receive:

With our store we worship Thee,
As we seek Thy favour free.

2. In the hollow of Thy hand
Is the wealth of sea and land;
All Thou grantest us to own
Appertains to Thee alone;
Claim, then claim, our earthly store
And ourselves for evermore!

3. In our wealth and poverty
With glad hearts we bow to Thee;
Thine we are in life, in death;
Thine from birth to latest breath;
Ransomed children, we shall be
Thine to all eternity.

4. Though our gifts be poor and small,
Thou dost welcome one and all;
Widow's mite or water cup,
To our Lord when offered up,
Is as precious in Thine eyes
As the costliest sacrifice.

5. Jesus, we our vows will pay
In Thy house on this Thy day;
And Thy service be our joy,
And Thy work our hands employ
Till we hear the sweet 'Well done'
From Thy glorious Judgment Throne.

254　　　　　　　　　　L. M.

" Of such is the kingdom of heaven."

1. A LITTLE child the Saviour came,
The mighty God was still His name
And angels worshipped, as He lay,
The seeming infant of a day.

2. He who, a little child, began
The life divine to show to man,
Proclaims from heaven the message free,
' Let little children come to Me.'

3. We bring them, Lord, and with the sign
Of sprinkled water name them Thine;
Their souls with saving grace endow,
Baptize them with Thy Spirit now.

4. O give Thine angels charge, good Lord!
Them safely in Thy way to guard;
Thy blessing on their lives command,
And write their names upon Thy hand.

5. O Thou, who by an infant's tongue
Dost hear Thy perfect glory sung,
May these, with all the heavenly host,
Praise Father, Son, and Holy Ghost.

255 C. M.

" He shall feed his flock like a shepherd."

1. SEE, Israel's gentle Shepherd stands,
With all-engaging charms;
Hark! how He calls the tender lambs,
And folds them in His arms.

2. Permit them to approach, He cries,
Nor scorn their humble name;
For 'twas to bless such souls as these
The Lord of angels came.

3. We bring them, Lord, in thankful hands,
And yield them up to Thee;
Joyful that we ourselves are Thine:
Thine let our offspring be.

256

C. M.

"This do in remembrance of me."

1. ACCORDING to Thy gracious word,
     In meek humility,
   This will I do, my dying Lord,
     I will remember Thee.

2. Thy body, broken for my sake,
     My bread from heaven shall be;
   Thy testamental cup I take,
     And thus remember Thee.

3. Gethsemane can I forget,
     Or there Thy conflict see,
   Thine agony and bloody sweat,
     And not remember Thee?

4. When to the cross I turn mine eyes,
     And gaze on Calvary,
   O Lamb of God, my sacrifice!
     I must remember Thee:—

5. Remember Thee, and all Thy pains,
     And all Thy love to me;
   Yea, while a breath, a pulse remains,
     Will I remember Thee.

6. And when these failing lips grow dumb,
     And mind and memory flee,
   When Thou shalt in Thy kingdom come,
     Then, Lord, remember me.

257   L. M.

" He brought me to the banqueting house."

1. MY God, and is Thy table spread,
   And does thy cup with love o'erflow?
Thither be all Thy children led,
   And let them all its sweetness know.

2. Hail, sacred feast, which Jesus makes,
   Rich banquet of His flesh and blood!
Thrice happy he who here partakes
   That sacred stream, that heavenly food!

3. O let Thy table honoured be,
   And furnished well with joyful guests;
And may each soul salvation see
   That here its sacred pledges tastes.

4. Let crowds approach with hearts prepared,
   With hearts inflamed let all attend;
Nor when we leave our Father's board,
   The pleasure or the profit end.

258   7s.

" The cup of blessing which we bless, is it not the communion of the blood of Christ? The bread which we break, is it not the communion of the body of Christ?"

1. JESUS, to Thy table led
   Now let every heart be fed
   With the true and living bread.

2. While upon Thy cross we gaze,
   Mourning o'er our sinful ways,
   Turn our sadness into praise.

3. When we taste the mystic wine,
   Of Thine outpoured blood the sign,
   Fill our hearts with love divine.

4. Draw us to Thy wounded side,
   Whence there flowed the healing tide;
   There our sins and sorrows hide.

5. From the bonds of sin release;
   Cold and wavering faith increase;
   Lamb of God, grant us Thy peace!

6. Lead us by Thy piercèd hand,
   Till around Thy throne we stand,
   In the bright and better land.

259   10s.

" Before whose eyes Jesus Christ hath been evidently set forth, crucified among you."

1. HERE, O my Lord, I see Thee face to face;
   Here faith can touch and handle things
      unseen;
   Here grasp with firmer hand the eternal grace,
   And all my weariness upon Thee lean.

2. Here would I feed upon the bread of God;
   Here drink with Thee the royal wine of
      heaven;
   Here would I lay aside each earthly load;
   Here taste afresh the calm of sin forgiven.

3. I have no help but Thine; nor do I need
   Another arm save Thine to lean upon;
   It is enough, my Lord, enough indeed;
   My strength is in Thy might, Thy might
      alone.

4. Mine is the sin, but Thine the righteousness;
    Mine is the guilt, but Thine the cleansing
        blood;
Here is my robe, my refuge, and my peace,
    Thy blood, Thy righteousness, O Lord my
        God.

5. Too soon we rise; the symbols disappear;
    The feast, though not the love, is past and
        gone;
The bread and wine remove, but Thou art here,
    Nearer than ever; still my Shield and Sun.

6. Feast after feast thus comes and passes by;
    Yet, passing, points to the glad feast above,
Giving sweet foretastes of the festal joy,
    The Lamb's great bridal feast of bliss and
        love.

260   C. M.

*"My flesh is meat indeed, and my blood
is drink indeed."*

1. O Jesus Christ, the Holy One,
    I long to be with Thee:
O Jesus Christ, the lowly One,
    Come and abide with me.

2. Now while the symbols of Thy love
    Before Thy saints are set,
And Thou, descending from above,
    Their yearning hearts hast met:

3. Come, and o'ershadow with Thy power
    This lonely heart of mine;
And feed me in this solemn hour
    With Thine own bread and wine.

4. My 'meat indeed,' my 'drink indeed,'
   Art Thou, my gracious Lord;
   Help Thou my soul by faith to feed
   On this Thy precious word,

5. Till nourished, strengthened, satisfied,
   My glad and thankful heart
   Forgets the things Thou hast denied
   In those Thou dost impart.

261   7s.

" Ye do show the Lord's death till he come."

1. 'TILL He come' — O let the words
   Linger on the trembling chords:
   Let the little while between
   In their golden light be seen;
   Let us think how heaven and home
   Lie beyond that ' Till He come.'

2. When the weary ones we love
   Enter on their rest above,
   Seems the earth so poor and vast,
   All our life-joy overcast?
   Hush, be every murmur dumb;
   It is only ' Till He come.'

3. Clouds and conflicts round us press:
   Would we have one sorrow less?
   All the sharpness of the cross,
   All that tells the world is loss,
   Death, and darkness, and the tomb,
   Only whisper ' Till He come.'

4. See, the feast of love is spread,
   Drink the wine, and break the bread:
   Sweet memorials, — till the Lord
   Call us round His heavenly board;
   Some from earth, from glory some,
   Severed only ' Till He come.'

262   L. M.

" All nations shall call him blessed."

1. JESUS shall reign where'er the sun
   Does his successive journeys run;
   His kingdom stretch from shore to shore,
   Till moons shall wax and wane no more.

2. For Him shall endless prayer be made,
   And praises throng to crown His head;
   His name like sweet perfume shall rise
   With every morning sacrifice.

3. People and realms of every tongue
   Dwell on His love with sweetest song;
   And infant voices shall proclaim
   Their early blessings on His name.

4. Blessings abound where'er He reigns;
   The prisoner leaps to lose his chains;
   The weary find eternal rest,
   And all the sons of want are blest.

5. Let every creature rise and bring
   Peculiar honours to our King;
   Angels descend with songs again,
   And earth repeat the loud Amen.

263   8, 7.

" Blessed be his glorious name for ever :
and let the whole earth be filled with
his glory. Amen, and amen."

1. ZION's King shall reign victorious,
   All the earth shall own His sway;
   He will make His kingdom glorious,
   He shall reign in endless day.

Nations now from God estrangèd,
  Then shall see a glorious light;
Night to day shall then be changèd,
  Heaven shall triumph in the sight.

2. Then shall Israel, long dispersèd,
  Mourning seek the Lord their God,
Look on Him whom once they piercèd,
  Own and kiss the chastening rod.
Mighty King, Thy arm revealing,
  Now Thy glorious cause maintain,
Bring the nations help and healing,
  Make them subject to Thy reign.

264   7, 6.

" O that the salvation of Israel were
come out of Zion !"

1. O THAT the Lord's salvation
    Were out of Zion come,
  To heal His ancient nation,
    To lead the outcasts home !

2. How long the holy city
    Shall heathen feet profane?
  Return, O Lord, in pity,
    Rebuild her walls again.

3. Let fall Thy rod of terror,
    Thy saving grace impart;
  Roll back the veil of error,
    Release the fettered heart.

4. Let Israel, home returning,
    Their lost Messiah see;
  Give oil of joy for mourning,
    And bind Thy Church to Thee.

265 L. M.

" Awake, awake, put on strength,
O arm of the Lord."

1. ARM of the Lord, awake, awake!
Put on Thy strength, the nations shake,
And let the world, adoring, see
Triumphs of mercy wrought by Thee.

2. Say to the heathen from Thy throne,
' I am Jehovah, God alone:'
Thy voice their idols shall confound,
And cast their altars to the ground.

3. Let Zion's time of favour come:
O bring the tribes of Israel home!
And let our wondering eyes behold
Gentiles and Jews in Jesus' fold.

4. Almighty God, Thy grace proclaim
In every clime of every name;
Let adverse powers before Thee fall,
And crown the Saviour Lord of all.

266 11, 10.

" He which converteth the sinner from
the error of his way shall save a
soul from death, and shall hide a
multitude of sins."

1. RESCUE the perishing, care for the dying,
Snatch them in pity from sin and the grave;
Weep o'er the erring one, lift up the fallen,
Tell them of Jesus, the Mighty to save.

Rescue the perishing, care for the dying,
Jesus is merciful, Jesus will save.

2. Though they are slighting Him, still He is wait-
 ing,
  Waiting the penitent child to receive:
 Plead with them earnestly, plead with them
  gently;
  He will forgive if they only believe.
   Rescue the perishing, &c.

3. Down in the human heart, crushed by the
 tempter,
  Feelings lie buried that grace can restore:
 Touched by a loving heart, wakened by kind-
  ness,
  Chords that were broken will vibrate once
  more.
   Rescue the perishing, &c.

4. Rescue the perishing, duty demands it,
  Strength for thy labour the Lord will provide:
 Back to the narrow way patiently win them;
  Tell the poor wanderer a Saviour has died.
   Rescue the perishing, &c.

267   P. M.

" He is become my salvation."

 1. SALVATION, O the joyful sound!
  'Tis pleasure to our ears,
 A sovereign balm for every wound,
  A cordial for our fears.

   Glory, honour, praise, and power
   Be unto the Lamb for ever!
   Jesus Christ is our Redeemer;
   Hallelujah! praise the Lord.

 2. Buried in sorrow and in sin,
  At hell's dark door we lay;

But we arise, by grace divine,
  To see a heavenly day.
     Glory, honour, &c.

3. Salvation! let the echo fly
  The spacious earth around,
While all the armies of the sky
  Conspire to raise the sound.
     Glory, honour, &c.

268   **7, 6.**

" In his days shall the righteous flourish."

1. HAIL to the Lord's Anointed!
  Great David's greater Son;
Hail, in the time appointed,
  His reign on earth begun.
He comes to break oppression,
  To set the captive free;
To take away transgression,
  And rule in equity.

2. He shall come down like showers
  Upon the fruitful earth;
And love, joy, hope, like flowers,
  Spring, in His path, to birth.
Before Him, on the mountains,
  Shall peace, the herald, go;
And righteousness, in fountains,
  From hill to valley flow.

3. Arabia's desert-ranger
  To him shall bow the knee;
The Ethiopian stranger
  His glory come to see:
With offerings of devotion,
  Ships from the isles shall meet
To pour the wealth of ocean
  In tribute at His feet.

4. Kings shall fall down before Him,
   And gold and incense bring;
All nations shall adore Him,
   His praise all people sing;
For He shall have dominion
   O'er river, sea, and shore,
Far as the eagle's pinion,
   Or dove's light wing, can soar.

5. For Him shall prayer unceasing
   And daily vows ascend;
His kingdom still increasing,
   A kingdom without end.
The mountain dews shall nourish
   A seed in weakness sown,
Whose fruit shall spread and flourish,
   And shake like Lebanon.

6. O'er every foe victorious,
   He on His throne shall rest;
From age to age more glorious,
   All blessing and all blest.
The tide of time shall never
   His covenant remove;
His name shall stand for ever;
   That name to us is Love.

269

7, 6.

"Come over . . . and help us."

1. FROM Greenland's icy mountains,
   From India's coral strand,
Where Afric's sunny fountains
   Roll down their golden sand,
From many an ancient river,
   From many a palmy plain,
They call us to deliver
   Their land from error's chain.

2. What though the spicy breezes
    Blow soft o'er Ceylon's isle;
Though every prospect pleases,
    And only man is vile;
In vain with lavish kindness
    The gifts of God are strown;
The heathen in his blindness
    Bows down to wood and stone.

3. Can we, whose souls are lighted
    With wisdom from on high,
Can we to men benighted
    The lamp of life deny?
Salvation, O salvation!
    The joyful sound proclaim,
Till each remotest nation
    Has learnt Messiah's name.

4. Waft, waft, ye winds, His story,
    And you, ye waters, roll,
Till, like a sea of glory,
    It spreads from pole to pole;
Till o'er our ransomed nature
    The Lamb for sinners slain,
Redeemer, King, Creator,
    In bliss returns to reign.

270   6, 4.

" God said, Let there be light ; and there
    was light."

1. THOU, whose Almighty word
Chaos and darkness heard,
    And took their flight,
Hear us, we humbly pray,
And where the gospel-day
Sheds not its glorious ray,
    Let there be light!

2. Thou, who didst come to bring
On Thy redeeming wing
  Healing and sight,
Health to the sick in mind,
Sight to the inly blind,
O now to all mankind
  Let there be light!

3. Spirit of truth and love,
Life-giving, holy Dove,
  Speed forth Thy flight;
Move on the waters' face,
Bearing the lamp of grace,
And in earth's darkest place
  Let there be light!

4. Holy and blessèd Three,
Glorious Trinity,
  Wisdom, Love, Might:
Boundless as ocean's tide,
Rolling in fullest pride,
Through the earth far and wide,
  Let there be light!

271   8, 7, 4.

*" The people which sat in darkness saw
  a great light."*

1. O'ER the gloomy hills of darkness,
  Look, my soul, be still and gaze;
All the promises do travail
  With a glorious day of grace:
    Blessed Jubilee,
  Let the glorious morning dawn.

2. Kingdoms wide that sit in darkness,
  Grant them, Lord, the glorious light,

And from eastern coast to western
    May the morning chase the night,
        And redemption,
    Freely purchased, win the day.

3. Fly abroad, thou mighty Gospel!
    Win and conquer, never cease ;
    May thy lasting, wide dominions
    Multiply, and still increase ;
        Sway Thy sceptre,
    Saviour all the world around.

272 C. M.

" Let all the people praise thee."

1. LIGHT of the lonely pilgrim's heart,
    Star of the coming day,
    Arise, and with Thy morning beams
    Chase all our griefs away.

2. Come, blessèd Lord ! bid every shore
    And answering island sing
    The praises of Thy royal name,
    And own Thee as their King.

3. Bid the whole earth responsive now
    To the bright world above,
    Break forth in rapturous strains of joy,
    In memory of Thy love.

4. Lord, Lord, Thy fair creation groans,
    The air, the earth, the sea,
    In unison with all our hearts,
    And calls aloud for Thee.

5. Come, then, with all Thy quickening power,
    With one awakening smile,
    And bid the serpent's trail no more
    Thy beauteous realms defile.

6. Thine was the cross, with all its fruits
 Of grace and peace divine :
Be Thine the crown of glory now
 The palm of victory Thine.

273   7s.

*" Alleluia ; for the Lord God omnipotent
reigneth."*

1. HARK! the song of Jubilee,
 Loud as mighty thunder's roar,
Or the fulness of the sea,
 When it breaks upon the shore :
Hallelujah! for the Lord
 God omnipotent shall reign :
Hallelujah! let the word
 Echo round the earth and main.

2. Hallelujah! hark! the sound,
 From the depths unto the skies,
Wakes above, beneath, around,
 All creation's harmonies ;
See Jehovah's banner furled,
 Sheathed His sword : He speaks, 'tis done ;
And the kingdoms of this world
 Are the kingdoms of His Son.

3. He shall reign from pole to pole,
 With illimitable sway ;
He shall reign, when like a scroll
 Yonder heavens have passed away :
Then the end; beneath His rod
 Man's last enemy shall fall :
Hallelujah! Christ in God,
 God in Christ, is all in all.

274   7s.

" That the word of the Lord may have
free course, and be glorified."

1. SPREAD, O spread, thou mighty word,
   Spread the kingdom of the Lord,
   Wheresoe'er His breath has given
   Life to beings meant for heaven.

2. Tell them how the Father's will
   Made the world and keeps it still,
   How He sent His Son to save
   All who help and comfort crave.

3. Tell of our Redeemer's love,
   Who for ever doth remove,
   By His holy sacrifice,
   All the guilt that on us lies.

4. Tell them of the Spirit given
   Now, to guide us up to heaven,
   Strong and holy, just and true, .
   Working both to will and do.

5. Word of Life! most pure and strong,
   Lo! for thee the nations long;
   Spread, till from its dreary night
   All the world awakes to light.

6. Up, the ripening fields ye see,
   Mighty shall the harvest be;
   But the reapers still are few,
   Great the work they have to do.

7. Lord of harvest, let there be
   Joy and strength to work for Thee;
   Let the nations far and near
   See Thy light and learn Thy fear.

275   6, 8.

" The acceptable year of the Lord."

1. BLOW ye the trumpet, blow
      The gladly solemn sound :
   Let all the nations know,
      To earth's remotest bound,
   The year of Jubilee is come ;
   Return, ye ransomed sinners, home.

2. Jesus, our great High Priest,
      Hath full atonement made ;
   Ye weary spirits, rest ;
      Ye mournful souls, be glad :
   The year of Jubilee is come ;
   Return, ye ransomed sinners, home.

3. Extol the Lamb of God,
      The all-atoning Lamb ;
   Redemption through His blood
      Throughout the world proclaim :
   The year of Jubilee is come ;
   Return, ye ransomed sinners, home.

4. Ye who have sold for nought
      Your heritage above,
   Receive it back unbought,
      The gift of Jesus' love :
   The year of Jubilee is come ;
   Return, ye ransomed sinners, home.

5. The Gospel trumpet hear,
      The news of heavenly grace ;
   And, saved from earth, appear
      Before your Saviour's face :
   The year of Jubilee is come ;
   Return, ye ransomed sinners, home.

VI. — *DEATH, RESURRECTION, HEAVEN.*

276   S. M.

" A little while."

1. A FEW more years shall roll,
   A few more seasons come ;
And we shall be with those that rest
   Asleep within the tomb.

   Then, O my Lord, prepare
      My soul for that great day ;
   O wash me in Thy precious blood,
      And take my sins away.

2. A few more suns shall set
   O'er these dark hills of time ;
And we shall be where suns are not,
   A far serener clime.
         Then, O my Lord, &c.

3. A few more storms shall beat
   On this wild rocky shore ;
And we shall be where tempests cease,
   And surges swell no more.
         Then, O my Lord, &c.

4. A few more Sabbaths here
   Shall cheer us on our way ;
And we shall reach the endless rest,
   The eternal Sabbath-day.
      Then, O my Lord, &c.

5. 'Tis but a little while,
    And He shall come again;
Who died that we might live, Who lives
That we with Him may reign.
        Then, O my Lord, &c.

277   6, 8.

" So shall we ever be with the Lord."

1. FRIEND after friend departs;
      Who hath not lost a friend?
There is no union here of hearts,
      That finds not here an end:
Were this frail world our only rest,
Living or dying, none were blest.

2. Beyond the flight of time,
      Beyond this vale of death,
There surely is some blessed clime,
      Where life is not a breath,
Nor life's affections transient fire,
Whose sparks fly upwards to expire.

3. There is a world above,
      Where parting is unknown;
A whole eternity of love,
      Formed for the good alone:
And faith beholds the dying here
Translated to that happier sphere.

4. Thus star by star declines
      Till all are passed away,
As morning high and higher shines
      To pure and perfect day;
Nor sink those stars in empty night;
They hide themselves in heaven's own light.

278   L. M.

"Lord, now lettest thou thy servant
depart in peace."

1. THE hour of my departure's come;
   I hear the voice that calls me home:
   At last, O Lord! let trouble cease,
   And let Thy servant die in peace.

2. The race appointed I have run;
   The combat's o'er, the prize is won;
   And now my witness is on high,
   And now my record's in the sky.

3. Not in mine innocence I trust;
   I bow before Thee in the dust;
   And through my Saviour's blood alone
   I look for mercy at Thy throne.

4. I leave the world without a tear,
   Save for the friends I hold so dear;
   To heal their sorrows, Lord, descend,
   And to the friendless prove a Friend.

5. I come, I come, at Thy command,
   I give my spirit to Thy hand;
   Stretch forth Thine everlasting arms,
   And shield me in the last alarms.

6. The hour of my departure's come;
   I hear the voice that calls me home:
   Now, O my God! let trouble cease;
   Now let Thy servant die in peace.

279   L. M.

*" Them also which sleep in Jesus, will
God bring with him."*

1. ASLEEP in Jesus! blessèd sleep,
   From which none ever wake to weep,
   A calm and undisturbed repose,
   Unbroken by the last of foes.

2. Asleep in Jesus! O how sweet
   To be for such a slumber meet,
   With holy confidence to sing
   That death hath lost its venomed sting!

3. Asleep in Jesus! peaceful rest,
   Whose waking is supremely blest;
   No fear, no woe shall dim that hour
   That manifests the Saviour's power.

4. Asleep in Jesus! O for me
   May such a blissful refuge be!
   Securely shall my ashes lie,
   Waiting the summons from on high.

5. Asleep in Jesus! time nor space
   Debars this precious hiding-place;
   On Indian plains or Lapland snows,
   Believers find the same repose.

6. Asleep in Jesus! far from thee
   Thy kindred and their graves may be,
   But thine is still a blessèd sleep,
   From which none ever wakes to weep.

280   7s.

*" When they had nothing to pay, he frankly
forgave them both."*

1. WHEN this passing world is done,
When has sunk yon glaring sun,
When we stand with Christ in glory,
Looking o'er life's finished story,
Then, Lord, shall I fully know —
Not till then — how much I owe.

2. When I stand before the throne,
Dressed in beauty not my own,
When I see Thee as Thou art,
Love Thee with unsinning heart,
Then, Lord, shall I fully know —
Not till then — how much I owe.

3. When the praise of heaven I hear,
Loud as thunders to the ear,
Loud as many waters' noise,
Sweet as harp's melodious voice,
Then, Lord, shall I fully know —
Not till then — how much I owe.

4. Chosen not for good in me,
Wakened up from wrath to flee,
Hidden in the Saviour's side,
By the Spirit sanctified,
Teach me, Lord, on earth to show,
By my love how much I owe.

281   7, 6.

" Thy land, O Immanuel."

1. THE sands of time are sinking,
The dawn of heaven breaks,
The summer morn I've sighed for,
The fair sweet morn awakes:

Dark, dark hath been the midnight,
  But day-spring is at hand,
And glory, glory dwelleth
  In Immanuel's land.

2. O Christ, He is the fountain,
    The deep sweet well of love;
  The streams on earth I've tasted,
    More deep I'll drink above.
  There to an ocean fulness
    His mercy doth expand,
  And glory, glory dwelleth
    In Immanuel's land.

3. With mercy and with judgment,
    My web of time He wove,
  And aye the dews of sorrow
    Were lustred with His love.
  I'll bless the hand that guided,
    I'll bless the heart that planned,
  When throned where glory dwelleth,
    In Immanuel's land.

4. O I am my Belovèd's,
    And my Belovèd's mine,
  He brings a poor vile sinner
    Into His ' house of wine.'
  I stand upon His merit;
    I know no other stand,
  Not e'en where glory dwelleth,
    In Immanuel's land.

282   S. M.

*" Whosoever liveth and believeth in me
    shall never die."*

1. It is not death to die,
    To leave this weary road,
  And, 'midst the brotherhood on high,
    To be at home with God.

2. It is not death to close
   The eye long dimmed by tears,
And wake in glorious repose,
   To spend eternal years.

3. It is not death to fling
   Aside this sinful dust,
And rise on strong, exulting wing,
   To live among the just.

4. Jesus, Thou Prince of life!
   Thy chosen cannot die;
Like Thee, they conquer in the strife,
   To reign with Thee on high.

283   S. M.

*" There remaineth, therefore, a rest to
the people of God."*

1. O WHERE shall rest be found,
   Rest for the weary soul?
'Twere vain the ocean's depths to sound,
   Or pierce to either pole.
   The world can never give
   The bliss for which we sigh;
'Tis not the whole of life to live,
   Nor all of death to die.

2. Beyond this vale of tears
   There is a life above,
Unmeasured by the flight of years,
   And all that life is love.
   There is a death whose pang
   Outlasts the fleeting breath;
O what eternal horrors hang
   Around the second death!

3. Lord God of truth and grace,
   Teach us that death to shun;
Lest we be banished from Thy face,
   And evermore undone.
   Here would we end our quest;
   Alone are found in Thee,
The life of perfect love — the rest
   Of immortality.

284   S. M.

" And the dead were judged."

1. THOU Judge of quick and dead,
   Before whose bar severe,
With holy joy, or guilty dread,
   We all shall soon appear;

2. Our cautioned souls prepare
   For that tremendous day,
And fill us now with watchful care,
   And stir us up to pray:

3. To pray, and wait the hour,
   That awful hour unknown,
When, robed in majesty and power,
   Thou shalt from heav'n come down,

4. Th' immortal Son of Man,
   To judge the human race,
With all Thy Father's dazzling train,
   With all Thy glorious grace!

5. O may we thus be found
   Obedient to His word,
Attentive to the trumpet's sound,
   And looking for our Lord!

285   8, 7.

" I saw the dead, small and great, stand
before God."

1. GREAT God, what do I see and hear!
    The end of things created!
  The Judge of mankind doth appear
    On clouds of glory seated!
  The trumpet sounds; the graves restore
  The dead which they contained before;
    Prepare, my soul, to meet Him!

2. The dead in Christ shall first arise,
    At the last trumpet's sounding;
  Caught up to meet Him in the skies,
    With joy their Lord surrounding:
  No gloomy fears their souls dismay;
  His presence sheds eternal day
    On those prepared to meet Him.

3. But sinners, filled with guilty fears,
    Behold His wrath prevailing;
  For they arise, and find their tears
    And sighs are unavailing.
  The day of grace is past and gone;
  Trembling they stand before the throne,
    All unprepared to meet Him.

4. Great God, what do I see and hear!
    The end of things created!
  The Judge of mankind doth appear
    On clouds of glory seated!
  Beneath His cross I view the day
  When heaven and earth shall pass away,
    And thus prepare to meet Him.

286

C. M.

*"Let me go over and see the good land
that is beyond Jordan."*

1. THERE is a land of pure delight,
    Where saints immortal reign,
  Infinite day excludes the night,
    And pleasures banish pain.

2. There everlasting spring abides,
    And never-withering flowers;
  Death, like a narrow sea, divides
    This heavenly land from ours.

3. Sweet fields beyond the swelling flood
    Stand dressed in living green;
  So to the Jews old Canaan stood,
    While Jordan rolled between.

4. But timorous mortals start and shrink
    To cross this narrow sea,
  And linger shivering on the brink,
    And fear to launch away.

5. O could we make our doubts remove,
    These gloomy doubts that rise,
  And see the Canaan that we love,
    With unbeclouded eyes;

6. Could we but climb where Moses stood,
    And view the landscape o'er,
  Not Jordan's stream, nor death's cold flood,
    Should fright us from the shore.

287
P. M.

" The inheritance of the saints in light."

1. WE speak of the realms of the blest,
    Of that country so bright and so fair,
And oft are its glories confessed ;
    But what must it be to be there ?

2. We speak of its pathways of gold,
    Of its walls decked with jewels so rare,
Its wonders and pleasures untold ;
    But what must it be to be there ?

3. We speak of its freedom from sin,
    From sorrow, temptation, and care,
From trials without and within ;
    But what must it be to be there ?

4. We speak of its service of love,
    The robes which the glorified wear,
The Church of the first-born above ;
    But what must it be to be there ?

5. Do Thou, Lord, 'midst pleasure or woe,
    Still for heaven our spirits prepare,
And shortly we also shall know
    And feel what it is to be there.

288
C. M.

*" Of whom the whole family in heaven
and earth is named."*

1. Come, let us join our friends above,
    That have obtained the prize,
And on the eagle wings of love
    To joys celestial rise.

248

Let all the saints terrestrial sing
  With those to glory gone,
For all the servants of our King,
  In earth and heaven, are one.

2. One family, we dwell in Him,
    One Church, above, beneath,
  Though now divided by the stream,
    The narrow stream of death.
  One army of the living God,
    To His command we bow;
  Part of His host hath crossed the flood,
    And part is crossing now.

3. Our old companions in distress
    We haste again to see,
  And eager long for our release
    And full felicity:
  Even now by faith we join our hands
    With those that went before,
  And greet the blood-besprinkled bands
    On the eternal shore.

4. Our spirits, too, shall quickly join,
    Like theirs with glory crowned,
  And shout to see our Captain's sign,
    To hear His trumpet sound.
  O that we now might grasp our Guide!
    O that the word were given!
  Come, Lord of hosts, the waves divide,
    And land us all in heaven.

289   P. M.

" We are journeying unto the place, of
which the Lord said, I will give
it you."

1. FROM Egypt lately come,
    Where death and darkness reign,

We seek our new, our better home,
Where we our rest shall gain.
Hallelujah!
We are on our way to God.

2. To Canaan's sacred bound
We haste with songs of joy;
Where peace and liberty are found,
And sweets that never cloy.
Hallelujah! — &c.

3. There sin and sorrow cease,
Aud every conflict's o'er;
There we shall dwell in endless peace,
And never hunger more.
Hallelujah! — &c.

4. There, in celestial strains,
Enraptured myriads sing;
There love in every bosom reigns,
For God Himself is King.
Hallelujah! — &c.

5. We soon shall join the throng,
Their pleasures we shall share,
And sing the everlasting song,
With all the ransomed there.
Hallelujah! — &c.

290   6s.

*" God shall wipe away all tears from
their eyes."*

1. THERE is a blessèd home
Beyond this land of woe,
Where trials never come,
Nor tears of sorrow flow;

Where faith is lost in sight,
  And patient hope is crowned,
And everlasting light
  Its glory throws around.

2. There is a land of peace,
  Good angels know it well;
Glad songs that never cease
  Within its portals swell;
Around its glorious throne
  Ten thousand saints adore
Christ, with the Father one,
  And Spirit, evermore.

3. O joy all joys beyond,
  To see the Lamb who died,
And count each sacred wound
  In hands and feet and side;
To give to Him the praise
  Of every triumph won,
And sing through endless days
  The great things He hath done.

4. Look up, ye saints of God,
  Nor fear to tread below
The path your Saviour trod
  Of daily toil and woe;
Wait but a little while
  In uncomplaining love,
His own most gracious smile
  Shall welcome you above.

6s.   **291**   7, 6.

from

" By reason of the glory that excelleth."

1. OH, fair the gleams of glory,
  And bright the scenes of mirth,
That lighten human story
  And cheer this weary earth;

But richer far our treasure
　With whom the Spirit dwells,
Ours, ours in heavenly measure
　The glory that excels.

2. The lamplight faintly gleameth
　　Where shines the noonday ray;
From Jesus' face there beameth
　Light of a sevenfold day;
And earth's pale lights, all faded,
　The Light from heaven dispels;
But shines for aye unshaded
　The glory that excels.

3. No broken cisterns need they
　　Who drink from living rills;
No other music heed they
　Whom God's own music thrills.
Earth's precious things are tasteless,
　Its boisterous mirth repels,
Where flows in measure wasteless
　The glory that excels.

4. Since on our life descended
　　Those beams of light and love,
Our steps have heavenward tended,
　Our eyes have looked above,
Till through the clouds concealing
　The home where glory dwells,
Our Jesus comes revealing
　The glory that excels.

292　　　　　　　　　　　　　　　S. M.

"And so shall we ever be with the Lord."

1. FOREVER with the Lord!
　Amen! so let it be;
Life from the dead is in that word,
　'Tis immortality.

Here in the body pent,
Absent from Him I roam,
Yet nightly pitch my moving tent
A day's march nearer home.

2. My Father's house on high,
Home of my soul, how near,
At times, to faith's foreseeing eye
Thy golden gates appear!
Ah! then my spirit faints
To reach the land I love,
The bright inheritance of saints,
Jerusalem above.

3. Forever with the Lord!
Father, if 'tis Thy will,
The promise of that faithful word
Even here to me fulfil.
Be Thou at my right hand,
Then can I never fail;
Uphold Thou me, and I shall stand;
Fight, and I must prevail.

4. So, when my latest breath
Shall rend the veil in twain,
By death I shall escape from death,
And life eternal gain.
Knowing as I am known,
How shall I love that word,
And oft repeat before the throne,
'Forever with the Lord!'

5. The trump of final doom
Will speak the self-same word,
And heaven's voice thunder through the tomb,
'Forever with the Lord!'
The tomb shall echo deep
That death-awakening sound;
The saints shall hear it in their sleep,
And answer from the ground.

6. Then, upward as they fly,
    That resurrection-word
Shall be their shout of victory,
    ' Forever with the Lord!'
    That resurrection-word,
    That shout of victory,
Once more, ' Forever with the Lord!'
    Amen! so let it be!

293   C. M.

" The holy city, New Jerusalem."

1. JERUSALEM, my happy home,
    Name ever dear to me:
When shall my labours have an end,
    In joy, and peace, and thee?

2. When shall these eyes thy heaven-built walls
    And pearly gates behold?
Thy bulwarks with salvation strong,
    And streets of shining gold?

3. There happier bowers than Eden's bloom,
    Nor sin nor sorrow know:
Blest seats! through rude and stormy scenes
    I onward press to you.

4. Why should I shrink from pain and woe,
    Or feel at death dismay?
I've Canaan's goodly land in view,
    And realms of endless day.

5. Apostles, martyrs, prophets, there
    Around my Saviour stand;
And soon my friends in Christ below
    Will join the glorious band.

6. Jerusalem, my happy home!
　My soul still pants for thee;
Then shall my labours have an end,
　When I thy joys shall see.

294　　　　　　　　　**7, 6.**

*"But now they desire a better country,
that is an heavenly."*

1. THE world is very evil,
　　The times are waxing late;
Be sober and keep vigil,
　　The Judge is at the gate, —
The Judge that comes in mercy,
　　The Judge that comes with might
To terminate the evil,
　　To diadem the right.

2. Then glory yet unheard of
　　Shall shed abroad its ray,
Resolving all enigmas,
　　An endless Sabbath-day.
Then, then from his oppressors
　　The Hebrew shall go free,
And celebrate in triumph
　　The year of Jubilee.

3. Then, nothing can be feeble,
　　There none can ever mourn,
There nothing is divided,
　　There nothing can be torn.
Strive, man, to win that glory;
　　Toil, man, to gain that light;
Send hope before to grasp it,
　　Till hope be lost in sight.

4. O sweet and blessèd country,
　　The home of God's elect!

O sweet and blessèd country,
That eager hearts expect!
Jesus, in mercy bring us
To that dear land of rest;
Who art, with God the Father,
And Spirit, ever blest.

295   7, 6.

" There shall be no more curse."

1. BRIEF life is here our portion;
    Brief sorrow, short-lived care;
The life that knows no ending,
    The tearless life, is there.
O happy retribution!
    Short toil, eternal rest;
For mortals and for sinners
    A mansion with the blest!

2. There grief is turned to pleasure,
    Such pleasure, as below
No human voice can utter,
    No human heart can know.
And now we fight the battle,
    But then shall wear the crown
Of full and everlasting
    And passionless renown.

3. And now we watch and struggle,
    And now we live in hope,
And Sion in her anguish
    With Babylon must cope;
But He whom now we trust in
    Shall then be seen and known,
And they that know and see Him
    Shall have Him for their own.

4. The morning shall awaken,
    The shadows shall decay,
And each true-hearted servant
    Shall shine as doth the day :
Yes; God, our King and Portion,
    In fulness of His grace,
We then shall see for ever,
    And worship face to face.

5. O sweet and blessèd country,
    The home of God's elect!
O sweet and blessèd country,
    That eager hearts expect!
Jesus, in mercy bring us
    To that dear land of rest;
Who art, with God the Father,
    And Spirit, ever blest.

296   7, 6.

" For he looked for a city which hath
*   foundations."*

1. FOR thee, O dear, dear country!
    Mine eyes their vigils keep;
For very love, beholding
    Thy happy name, they weep:
The mention of thy glory
    Is unction to the breast,
And medicine in sickness,
    And love, and life, and rest.

2. O one, O only mansion!
    O Paradise of joy!
Where tears are ever banished,
    And smiles have no alloy:
With jaspers glow thy bulwarks;
    Thy streets with emeralds blaze ·
The sardius and the topaz
    Unite in thee their rays :

3. Thine ageless walls are bonded
    With amethyst unpriced;
  The saints build up its fabric,
    And the corner-stone is Christ.
  The cross is all thy splendour,
    The Crucified thy praise:
  His laud and benediction
    Thy ransomed people raise.

4. Thou hast no shore, fair ocean!
    Thou hast no time, bright day!
  Dear fountain of refreshment,
    To pilgrims far away:
  Upon the Rock of Ages
    They raise thy holy tower:
  Thine is the victor's laurel,
    And thine the golden dower.

5. O sweet and blessèd country,
    The home of God's elect!
  O sweet and blessèd country,
    That eager hearts expect!
  Jesus, in mercy bring us
    To that dear land of rest;
  Who art, with God the Father,
    And Spirit, ever blest.

297   **7, 6.**

"The city was pure gold, like unto clear glass."

1. JERUSALEM the golden,
    With milk and honey blest,
  Beneath thy contemplation
    Sink heart and voice opprest:
  I know not, O, I know not,
    What joys await us there;
  What radiancy of glory,
    What light beyond compare!

2. They stand, those halls of Sion,
　All jubilant with song,
And bright with many an angel,
　And all the martyr throng;
The Prince is ever in them;
　The daylight is serene;
The pastures of the blessèd
　Are decked in glorious sheen.

3. There is the throne of David;
　And there, from care released,
The shout of them that triump',
　The song of them that feast;
And they who, with their Le.der,
　Have conquered in the fig't,
For ever and for ever
　Are clad in robes of white.

4. O sweet and blessèd country,
　The home of God's elect!
O sweet and blessèd country,
　That eager hearts expect!
Jesus, in mercy bring us
　To that dear land of rest;
Who art, with God the Father,
　And Spirit, ever blest.

, 6.

clear

VII. — *MISCELLANEOUS.*

298 L. M.

"My voice shalt thou hear in the morning, O Lord."

1. AWAKE, my soul, and with the sun
   Thy daily stage of duty run;
   Shake off dull sloth, and joyful rise
   To pay thy morning sacrifice.

2. Thy precious time misspent redeem;
   Each present day thy last esteem;
   Improve thy talent with due care;
   For the great day thyself prepare.

3. In conversation be sincere;
   Keep conscience as the noontide clear;
   Think how All-seeing God thy ways
   And all thy secret thoughts surveys.

4. Wake, and lift up thyself, my heart,
   And with the angels bear thy part,
   Who, all night long, unwearied sing
   High praise to the eternal King.

5. All praise to Thee who safe hast kept,
   And hast refreshed me whilst I slept:
   Grant, Lord, when I from death shall wake,
   I may of endless light partake.

6. Lord, I my vows to Thee renew;
Disperse my sins as morning dew;
Guard my first springs of thought and will,
And with Thyself my spirit fill.

7. Direct, control, suggest, this day,
All I design, or do, or say;
That all my powers, with all their might,
In Thy sole glory may unite.

8. Praise God, from whom all blessings flow;
Praise Him, all creatures here below;
Praise Him above, ye heavenly host;
Praise Father, Son, and Holy Ghost.

299

L. M.

"His compassions fail not : they are new every morning."

1. O TIMELY happy, timely wise,
Hearts that with rising morn arise !
Eyes that the beam celestial view,
Which evermore makes all things new.

2. New every morning is the love
Our wakening and uprising prove:
Through sleep and darkness safely brought,
Restored to life, and power, and thought.

3. New mercies, each returning day,
Hover around us while we pray;
New perils past, new sins forgiven,
New thoughts of God, new hopes of heaven.

4. If, on our daily course, our mind
Be set to hallow all we find,
New treasures still, of countless price,
God will provide for sacrifice.

5. The trivial round, the common task,
   Will furnish all we ought to ask;
   Room to deny ourselves; a road
   To bring us daily nearer God.

6. Only, O Lord, in Thy dear love,
   Fit us for perfect rest above;
   And help us, this and every day,
   To live more nearly as we pray.

300 7s.

" The dayspring from on high hath visited us."

1. CHRIST, whose glory fills the skies,
       Christ, the true, the only Light,
   Sun of righteousness, arise,
       Triumph o'er the shades of night!
   Day-spring from on high, be near;
       Day-star, in my heart appear.

2. Dark and cheerless is the morn
       Unaccompanied by Thee;
   Joyless is the day's return,
       Till Thy mercy's beams I see;
   Till they inward light impart,
   Glad my eyes, and warm my heart.

3. Visit then this soul of mine,
       Pierce the gloom of sin and grief;
   Fill me, Radiancy Divine,
       Scatter all my unbelief:
   More and more Thyself display,
   Shining to the perfect day!

801

" Thou, Lord, only makest me dwell in safety."

1. ALL praise to Thee, my God, this night,
   For all the blessings of the light;
   Keep me, O keep me, King of kings,
   Beneath Thine own almighty wings!

2. Forgive me, Lord, for Thy dear Son,
   The ill that I this day have done;
   That, with the world, myself, and Thee,
   I, ere I sleep, at peace may be.

3. Teach me to live, that I may dread
   The grave as little as my bed;
   Teach me to die, that so I may
   Rise glorious at the judgment-day.

4. O may my soul on Thee repose,
   And may sweet sleep mine eyelids close;
   Sleep that may me more vigorous make,
   To serve my God when I awake.

5. When in the night I sleepless lie,
   My soul with heavenly thoughts supply;
   Let no ill dreams disturb my rest,
   No powers of darkness me molest.

6. Praise God, from whom all blessings flow;
   Praise Him, all creatures here below;
   Praise Him above, ye heavenly host;
   Praise Father, Son, and Holy Ghost.

263

302

L. M.

" Abide with us."

1. SUN of my soul, Thou Saviour dear!
   It is not night if Thou be near;
   O may no earth-born cloud arise,
   To hide Thee from Thy servant's eyes!

2. When the soft dews of kindly sleep
   My wearied eyelids gently steep,
   Be my last thought, how sweet to rest
   For ever on my Saviour's breast!

3. Abide with me from morn till eve,
   For without Thee I cannot live;
   Abide with me when night is nigh,
   For without Thee I dare not die.

4. If some poor wandering child of Thine
   Have spurned to-day the voice divine,
   Now, Lord, the gracious work begin,
   Let him no more lie down in sin.

5. Watch by the sick, enrich the poor
   With blessings from Thy boundless store;
   Be every mourner's sleep to-night,
   Like infant's slumbers, pure and light.

6. Come near and bless us when we wake,
   Ere through the world our way we take,
   Till, in the ocean of Thy love,
   We lose ourselves in heaven above.

303   8, 4.

" The Lord will command his loving-
kindness in the day-time, and in
the night his song shall be with
me."

1. GOD, that madest earth and heaven,
      Darkness and light;
Who the day for toil hast given,
      For rest the night;
May Thine angel-guards defend us!
Slumber sweet Thy mercy send us!
Holy dreams and hopes attend us,
      This livelong night!

2. Guard us waking, guard us sleeping;
      And, when we die,
May we, in Thy mighty keeping,
      All peaceful lie!
When the last dread trump shall wake us,
Do not Thou, our God, forsake us;
But to reign in glory take us
      With Thee on high.

304   8, 7.

" He shall give his angels charge over thee."

1. SAVIOUR, breathe an evening blessing,
      Ere repose our spirits seal;
Sin and want we come confessing:
      Thou canst save, and Thou canst heal
Though destruction walk around us,
      Though the arrows past us fly,
Angel-guards from Thee surround us;
      We are safe, if Thou art nigh.

2. Though the night be dark and dreary,
    Darkness cannot hide from Thee:
Thou art He, who, never weary,
    Watchest where Thy people be.
Should swift death this night o'ertake us,
    And our couch become our tomb,
May the morn in heaven awake us,
    Clad in light and deathless bloom.

305

8, 6.

" He is thy life and the length of thy days."

1. ANOTHER year hath fled; renew,
    Lord, with our days Thy love!
Our days are evil here and few;
    We look to live above:
We will not grieve, though day by day
We pass from earthly joys away;
    Our joy abides in Thee.

2. Yet, when our sins we call to mind,
    We cannot fail to grieve;
But Thou art pitiful and kind,
    And wilt our prayer receive:
O Jesus, evermore the same,
Our hope we rest upon Thy name;
    Our hope abides in Thee.

3. For all the future, Lord, prepare
    Our souls with strength divine;
Help us to cast on Thee our care,
    And on Thy servants shine:
Life without Thee is dark and drear;
Death is not death if Thou art near;
    Our life abides in Thee.

306   7s.

"Great is thy faithfulness."

1. FOR Thy mercy and Thy grace,
    Constant through another year,
Hear our song of thankfulness,
    Father and Redeemer, hear.

2. Lo! our sins on Thee we cast,
    Thee, our perfect sacrifice,
And, forgetting all the past,
    Press towards our glorious prize.

3. Dark the future: let Thy light
    Guide us, bright and morning Star:
Fierce our foes, and hard the fight;
    Arm us, Saviour, for the war.

4. In our weakness and distress,
    Rock of strength, be Thou our stay;
In the pathless wilderness
    Be our true and living way.

5. Who of us death's awful road
    In the coming year shall tread?
With Thy rod and staff, O God,
    Comfort Thou his dying bed.

6. Keep us faithful; keep us pure;
    Keep us evermore Thine own:
Help, O help us to endure;
    Fit us for the promised crown.

7. So within Thy palace gate
    We shall praise, on golden strings,
Thee, the only Potentate,
    Lord of lords, and King of kings.

307 7s.

*" So teach us to number our days, that
we may apply our hearts unto wisdom."*

1. WHILE with ceaseless course the sun
    Hasted through the former year;
Many souls their race have run,
    Never more to meet us here:
Fixed in an eternal state,
    They have done with all below
We a little longer wait,
    But how little, none can know.

2. As the wingèd arrow flies,
    Speedily the mark to find;
As the lightning from the skies
    Darts, and leaves no trace behind:
Swiftly thus our fleeting days
    Bear us down life's rapid stream;
Upwards, Lord, our spirits raise:
    All below is but a dream.

3. Thanks for mercies past receive;
    Pardon of our sins renew;
Teach us, henceforth, how to live
    With eternity in view:
Bless Thy word to young and old;
    Fill us with a Saviour's love;
And, when life's short tale is told,
    May we dwell with Thee above!

308 8, 7.

" As thy days, so shall thy strength be."

1. AT Thy feet, our God and Father,
    Who hast blest us all our days,
We with grateful hearts would gather,
    To begin the year with praise;—

Praise for light so brightly shining
  On our steps from heaven above ;
Praise for mercies daily twining
  Round us golden cords of love.

2. Jesus, for Thy love most tender
  On the cross for sinners shown,
We would praise Thee, and surrender
  All our hearts to be Thine own.
With so blest a Friend provided,
  We upon our way would go,
Sure of being safely guided,
  Guarded well from every foe.

3. Every day will be the brighter,
  When Thy gracious face we see ;
Every burden will be lighter,
  When we know it comes from Thee.
Spread thy love's broad banner o'er us,
  Give us strength to serve and wait,
Till Thy glory breaks before us,
  Through the city's open gate.

309
L. M.

*" Thou crownest the year with thy good-
  ness."*

1. ETERNAL Source of every joy,
  Well may Thy praise our lips employ,
While in Thy temple we appear,
  Whose goodness crowns the circling year.

2. The flowery spring at Thy command
  Embalms the air, and paints the land ;
The summer rays with vigour shine,
  To raise the corn, and cheer the vine.

269

3. Thy hand in autumn richly pours
   Through all our coasts redundant stores,
   And winters, softened by Thy care,
   No more a face of horror wear.

4. Seasons, and months, and weeks, and days,
   Demand successive songs of praise;
   Still be the cheerful homage paid,
   With opening light, and evening shade!

5. O may our more harmonious tongues
   In worlds unknown pursue the songs;
   And in those brighter courts adore,
   Where days and years revolve no more!

310   8s.

" Thou preparest them corn."

1. LORD of the harvest, once again
   We thank Thee for the ripened grain,
   For crops safe carried, sent to cheer
   Thy servants through another year;
   For all sweet holy thoughts, supplied
   By seed-time and by harvest-tide.

2. The bare dead grain, in autumn sown,
   Its robe of vernal green puts on;
   Glad from its wintry grave it springs,
   Fresh garnished by the King of kings;
   So, Lord, to those who sleep in Thee,
   Shall new and glorious bodies be.

3. Nor vainly of Thy word we ask
   A lesson from the reaper's task;
   So shall Thine angels issue forth;
   The tares be burnt; the just of earth,
   Playthings of sun and storm no more,
   Be gathered to their Father's store.

4. Daily, O Lord, our prayers be said,
As Thou hast taught, for daily bread;
But not alone our bodies feed,
Supply our fainting spirits' need:
O Bread of life, from day to day,
Be Thou their comfort, food, and stay.

311   7s.

" Let both grow together until harvest."

1. COME, ye thankful people, come,
Raise the song of Harvest-home:
All is safely gathered in,
Ere the winter storms begin:
God, our Maker, doth provide
For our wants to be supplied;
Come to God's own temple, come,
Raise the song of Harvest-home!

2. We ourselves are God's own field,
Fruit unto His praise to yield;
Wheat and tares together sown,
Unto joy or sorrow grown:
First the blade, and then the ear,
Then the full corn shall appear:
Grant, O harvest Lord, that we
Wholesome grain and pure may be.

3. For the Lord, our God, shall come,
And shall take His harvest home;
From His field shall in that day
All offences purge away:
Give His angels charge at last
In the fire the tares to cast;
But the fruitful ears to store
In His garner evermore.

4. Then, thou Church triumphant, come,
Raise the song of Harvest-home!
All are safely gathered in,
Free from sorrow, free from sin;
There, for ever purified,
In God's garner to abide:
Come, ten thousand angels, come,
Raise the glorious Harvest-home!

312

C. M.

" While the earth remaineth seed-time
and harvest . . . shall not cease."

1. FOUNTAIN of mercy, God of love,
    How rich Thy bounties are!
The rolling seasons, as they move,
    Proclaim Thy constant care.

2. When in the bosom of the earth
    The sower hid the grain,
Thy goodness marked its secret birth,
    And sent the early rain.

3. The spring's sweet influence was Thine;
    The plants in beauty grew;
Thou gav'st refulgent suns to shine,
    And mild refreshing dew.

4. These various mercies from above
    Matured the swelling grain;
A yellow harvest crowns Thy love,
    And plenty fills the plain.

5. Seed-time and harvest, Lord, alone
    Thou dost on man bestow;
Let him not then forget to own
    From whom his blessings flow.

6. Fountain of love, our praise is Thine;
   To Thee our songs we'll raise,
And all created nature join
   In sweet, harmonious praise.

313 P. M.

" Thou blessest the springing thereof."

1. WE plough the fields and scatter
      The good seed on the land,
   But it is fed and watered
      By God's Almighty hand:
   He sends the snow in winter,
      The warmth to swell the grain,
   The breezes and the sunshine,
      And soft refreshing rain.
         All good gifts around us
         Are sent from heaven above;
   Then thank the Lord, O thank the Lord,
         For all His love.

2. He only is the Maker
      Of all things near and far;
   He paints the wayside flower,
      He lights the evening star;
   The winds and waves obey Him,
      By Him the birds are fed;
   Much more to us, His children,
      He gives our daily bread.
         All good gifts around us
         Are sent from heaven above;
   Then thank the Lord, O thank the Lord,
         For all His love.

3. We thank Thee, then, O Father,
      For all things bright and good,
   The seed-time and the harvest,
      Our life, our health, our food;

273

No gifts have we to offer,
　For all Thy love imparts,
But that which Thou desirest,
　Our humble, thankful hearts.
　　All good gifts around us
　　Are sent from heaven above;
Then thank the Lord, O thank the Lord,
　For all His love.

314   8s.

" These see the works of the Lord, and his
wonders in the deep."

1. ETERNAL Father, strong to save,
Whose arm hath bound the restless wave,
Who bidd'st the mighty ocean deep
Its own appointed limits keep;
　O hear us when we cry to Thee
　For those in peril on the sea.

2. O Christ, whose voice the waters heard,
And hushed their raging at Thy word,
Who walkedst on the foaming deep,
And calm amidst its rage didst sleep;
　O hear us when we cry to Thee
　For those in peril on the sea.

3. Most Holy Spirit, who didst brood
Upon the chaos dark and rude,
And bid its angry tumult cease,
And give for wild confusion, peace;
　O hear us when we cry to Thee
　For those in peril on the sea.

4. O Trinity of love and power,
Our brethren shield in danger's hour;
From rock and tempest, fire and foe,
Protect them wheresoe'er they go;
　Thus evermore shall rise to Thee
　Glad hymns of praise from land and sea.

274

315

L. M.

*" Will ye not tremble at my presence,
which have placed the sand for the
bound of the sea ?"*

1. O GOD, who metest in Thine hand
   The waters of the mighty sea,
   And barrest ocean with the sand
   By Thy perpetual decree ;

2. What time the floods lift up their voice,
   And break in anger on the shore,
   When deep to deep calls with the noise
   Of waterspouts and billows' roar ;

3. When they who to the sea go down,
   And in the waters ply their toil,
   Are lifted on the surge's crown,
   And plunged where seething eddies boil ;

4. Rule then, O Lord, the ocean's wrath,
   And bind the tempest with Thy will ;
   Tread, as of old, the water's path,
   And speak Thy bidding, ' Peace, be still.'

5. So with Thy mercies ever new
   Thy servants set from peril free,
   And bring them, Pilot wise and true,
   Unto the port where they would be.

316

I IS.

*" Every good gift, and every perfect gift
is from above."*

1. THOU, Lord, art our life and the length of our
   days :
   Our voices to Thee in thanksgiving we raise ;
   Our shield and our buckler, our refuge and
   tower,
   We trust in Thy faithfulness, mercy, and power.

IMAGE EVALUATION
TEST TARGET (MT-3)

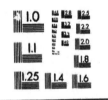

6"

Photographic
Sciences
Corporation

23 WEST MAIN STREET
WEBSTER, N.Y. 14580
(716) 872-4503

2. We thank Thee, we praise Thee, for sunshine
   and rain,
   For calm and for tempest, for pleasure and pain;
   Thy love and Thy wisdom our tongues shall
   employ,
   In light and in darkness, in sorrow and joy.

3. The summer and autumn, the winter and spring,
   To Thee shall their tribute of gratitude bring;
   The sea and its fulness, the earth and the air,
   All tell of Thy goodness, Thy glory declare.

4. We thank Thee, we praise Thee, for beauty and
   youth,
   For justice and freedom, for honour and truth;
   For the wealth of the ocean, the forest and field,
   And all the rewards that our industries yield.

5. We thank Thee, we praise Thee, for plenty and
   peace,
   For Thy full-flowing bounty that never doth
   cease,
   For the Church and the Sabbath, the Home and
   the School;
   For a land in which mercy and righteousness
   rule.

6. We thank Thee and praise Thee, our Father
   above,
   For all the dear tokens of kindness and love
   Thou sendest to greet us, as day follows day,
   To lighten our burdens and gladden our way.

7. We thank Thee for life with its blessings so free,
   And for the glad hope which we have, Lord, in
   Thee,
   That Thou wilt receive us in peace to Thy rest,
   To serve Thee on high with the saved and the
   blest.

317 7, 6.

"*Happy is that people whose God is the Lord.*"

1. FROM ocean unto ocean
   Our land shall own Thee Lord,
And, filled with true devotion,
   Obey Thy sovereign word.
Our prairies and our mountains,
   Forest and fertile field,
Our rivers, lakes, and fountains,
   To Thee shall tribute yield.

2. O Christ, for Thine own glory,
   And for our country's weal,
We humbly plead before Thee,
   Thyself in us reveal;
And may we know, Lord Jesus,
   The touch of Thy dear hand;
And, healed of our diseases,
   The tempter's power withstand.

3. Where error smites with blindness,
   Enslaves and leads astray,
Do Thou in loving kindness
   Proclaim Thy gospel day;
Till all the tribes and races
   That dwell in this fair land,
Adorned with Christian graces,
   Within Thy courts shall stand.

4. Our Saviour King, defend us,
   And guide where we should go;
Forth with Thy message send us,
   Thy love and light to show;
Till fired with true devotion
   Enkindled by Thy Word,
From ocean unto ocean
   Our land shall own Thee Lord.

318

" Remember, O Lord, what is come upon us; consider and behold our re-proach."

1. GREAT King of nations, hear our prayer,
   While at Thy feet we fall,
And humbly, with united cry,
   To Thee for mercy call;
The guilt is ours, but grace is Thine,
   O turn us not away,
But hear us from Thy lofty throne,
   And help us when we pray.

2. Our fathers' sins were manifold,
   And ours no less we own,
Yet wondrously from age to age
   Thy goodness hath been shown;
When dangers, like a stormy sea,
   Beset our country round,
To Thee we looked, to Thee we cried,
   And help in Thee we found:

3. With one consent we meekly bow
   Beneath Thy chast'ning hand,
And, pouring forth confession meet,
   Mourn with our mourning land;
With pitying eye behold our need,
   As thus we lift our prayer,
'Correct us with Thy judgments, Lord,
   Then let Thy mercy spare.'

319

" The place of my fathers' sepulchres."

1. LORD, while for all mankind we pray,
   Of every clime and coast,
O hear us for our native land,
   The land we love the most.

2. Our fathers' sepulchres are here,
   And here our kindred dwell;
   Our children, too;—how should we love
   Another land so well?

3. O guard our shores from every foe,
   With peace our borders bless;
   With prosperous times our cities crown,
   Our fields with plenteousness.

4. Unite us in the sacred love
   Of knowledge, truth, and Thee;
   And let our hills and valleys shout
   The songs of liberty.

5. Lord of the nations, thus to Thee
   Our country we commend;
   Be Thou our refuge and our trust,
   Our everlasting Friend.

320 L. M.

*" He maketh wars to cease unto the ends
of the earth."*

1. O GOD of love, O King of peace!
   Make wars throughout the world to cease;
   The wrath of sinful man restrain,
   Give peace, O God, give peace again!

2. Remember, Lord, Thy works of old,
   The wonders that our fathers told;
   Remember not our sin's dark stain,
   Give peace, O God, give peace again!

3. Whom shall we trust but Thee, O Lord?
   Where rest but on Thy faithful word?
   None ever called on Thee in vain,
   Give peace, O God, give peace again!

4. Where saints and angels dwell above,
   All hearts are knit in holy love;
   O bind us in that heavenly chain,
   Give peace, O God, give peace again.

321   8, 7.

" Suffer little children to come unto me."

1. LORD, a little band and lowly,
      We are come to sing to Thee;
   Thou art great, and high, and holy,
      O how solemn we should be!

2. Fill our hearts with thoughts of Jesus,
      And of heaven, where He is gone;
   And let nothing ever please us
      He would grieve to look upon.

3. For we know the Lord of glory
      Always sees what children do,
   And is writing now the story
      Of our thoughts and actions too.

4. Let our sins be all forgiven;
      Make us fear whate'er is wrong;
   Lead us on our way to heaven,
      There to sing a nobler song.

322   6s.

" Out of the mouth of babes and suck-
lings thou hast perfected praise."

1. COME, children, join to sing,
                  Hallelujah! Amen!
   Loud praise to Christ our King,
                  Hallelujah! Amen!
   Let all with heart and voice
   Before His throne rejoice;
   Praise is His gracious choice:
                  Hallelujah! Amen!

2. Come, lift your hearts on high;
     Hallelujah! Amen!
 Let praises fill the sky;
     Hallelujah! Amen!
 He is our guide and friend;
 To us He'll condescend;
 His love shall never end:
     Hallelujah! Amen!

3. Praise yet the Lord again;
     Hallelujah! Amen!
 Life shall not end the strain;
     Hallelujah! Amen!
 On heaven's blissful shore
 His goodness we'll adore,
 Singing for evermore,
     Hallelujah! Amen!

323   8, 6.

" Of such is the kingdom of heaven."

1. AROUND the throne of God in heaven
 Thousands of children stand,
 Whose sins are all through Christ forgiven,
 A holy, happy band,
  Singing, Glory, glory, glory!

2. What brought them to that world above,
 That heaven so bright and fair,
 Where all is peace and joy and love, —
 How came those children there,
  Singing, Glory, glory, glory?

3. Because the Saviour shed His blood
 To wash away their sin,
 Bathed in that pure and precious flood,
 Behold them white and clean,
  Singing, Glory, glory, glory!

4. On earth they sought the Saviour's grace,
    On earth they loved His name;
And now they see His blessèd face,
    And stand before the Lamb:
        Singing, Glory, glory, glory!

324   C, M.

" Remember now thy Creator in the days
of thy youth."

1. By cool Siloam's shady rill,
    How sweet the lily grows!
How sweet the breath beneath the hill
    Of Sharon's dewy rose!

2. Lo, such the child whose early feet
    The paths of peace have trod,
Whose secret heart with influence sweet
    Is upward drawn to God.

3. By cool Siloam's shady rill
    The lily must decay;
The rose that blooms beneath the hill
    Must shortly fade away.

4. And soon, too soon, the wintry hour
    Of man's maturer age
Will shake the soul with sorrow's power,
    And stormy passions rage.

5. O Thou, whose infant feet were found
    Within Thy Father's shrine,
Whose years, with changeless virtue crowned,
    Were all alike divine, —

6. Dependent on Thy bounteous breath,
    We seek Thy grace alone —
In childhood, manhood, age, and death,
    To keep us still Thine own!

325

C. M.

*" The Lord shall be thy confidence, and
shall keep thy foot from being taken."*

1. THE morning bright with rosy light
   Has waked me from my sleep;
   Father, I own Thy love alone
   Thy little one doth keep.

2. All through the day, I humbly pray,
   Be Thou my guard and guide;
   My sins forgive, and let me live,
   Lord Jesus, near Thy side.

3. O make Thy rest within my breast,
   Great Spirit of all grace;
   Make me like Thee, then shall I be
   Prepared to see Thy face.

326

8, 7.

*" He shall gather the lambs with his arm,
and carry them in his bosom."*

1. JESUS, tender Shepherd, hear me;
   Bless Thy little lamb to-night;
   Through the darkness be Thou near me;
   Watch my sleep till morning light.

2. All this day Thy hand has led me,
   And I thank Thee for Thy care;
   Thou hast clothed me, warmed and fed me;
   Listen to my evening prayer.

3. Let my sins be all forgiven;
   Bless the friends I love so well;
   Take me, when I die, to heaven,
   Happy there with Thee to dwell.

327

7, 6.

*" There is a friend that sticheth closer
than a brother."*

1. THERE's a Friend for little children
   Above the bright blue sky,
   A Friend that never changes,
   Whose love will never die:
   Unlike our friends by nature,
   Who change with changing years,
   This Friend is always worthy
   The precious name he bears.

2. There's a rest for little children
   Above the bright blue sky,
   Who love the blessèd Saviour
   And to His Father cry, —
   A rest from every trouble,
   From sin and danger free;
   There every little pilgrim
   Shall rest eternally.

3. There's a home for little children
   Above the bright blue sky,
   Where Jesus reigns in glory,
   A home of peace and joy;
   No home on earth is like it,
   Nor can with it compare,
   For every one is happy,
   Nor can be happier, there.

4. There's a crown for little children
   Above the bright blue sky,
   And all who look to Jesus
   Shall wear it by-and-by, —
   A crown of brightest glory,
   Which God shall then bestow
   On all who love the Saviour,
   And walk with Him below.

" Ye shall find the babe wrapped in swaddling clothes, lying in a manger."

1. ONCE in royal David's city
   Stood a lowly cattle-shed,
Where a mother laid her infant
   In a manger for His bed;
Mary was that mother mild,
Jesus Christ her little child.

2. He came down to earth from heaven
      Who is God and Lord of all,
   And His shelter was a stable,
      And His cradle was a stall;
With the poor, and mean, and lowly
Lived on earth our Saviour holy.

3. And, through all His wondrous childhood,
      He would honour and obey,
   Love, and watch the lowly mother
      In whose gentle arms He lay;
Christian children all should be
Mild, obedient, good as He.

4. For He is our childhood's pattern,
      Day by day like us He grew,
   He was little, weak, and helpless,
      Tears and smiles like us He knew;
And He feeleth for our sadness,
And He shareth in our gladness.

5. And our eyes at last shall see Him,
      Through His own redeeming love,
   For that Child so dear and gentle
      Is our Lord in heaven above;
And He leads His children on
To the place where He is gone.

6. Not in that poor lowly stable,
 With the oxen standing by,
We shall see Him; but in heaven,
 Set at God's right hand on high;
When like stars His children crowned
All in white shall wait around.

329   P. M.

*" Unto you is born this day, in the city of
 David, a Saviour which is Christ
 the Lord."*

1. THERE came a little Child to earth
   Long ago;
And the angels of God proclaimed His birth,
   High and low.

2. Out in the night, so calm and still,
   Their song was heard;
For they knew that the Child on Bethlehem's hill
   Was Christ the Lord.

3. Far away in a goodly land,
   Fair and bright,
Children with crowns of glory stand,
   Robed in white.

4. They sing how the Lord of that world so fair
   A child was born;
And, that they might His crown of glory share,
   Wore a crown of thorn;

5. And in mortal weakness, in want and pain,
   Came forth to die,
That the children of earth might in glory reign
   With Him on high.

5. And for evermore, in their robes so fair
  And undefiled,
Those ransomed children His praise declare,
  Who was once a child.

330   C. M.

" Hosanna in the highest."

1. HOSANNA! raise the joyful hymn
    To David's Son and Lord;
  With cherubim and seraphim
    Exalt the Incarnate Word.
  Hosanna! Lord, our feeble tongue
    No lofty strains can raise;
  But Thou wilt not despise the young,
    Who meekly chant Thy praise.

2. Hosanna! Sovereign, Prophet, Priest,
    How vast Thy gifts, how free!
  Thy blood, our life; Thy word, our feast;
    Thy name our only plea.
  Hosanna! Master, lo! we bring
    Our offerings to Thy throne;
  Not gold, nor myrrh, nor mortal thing,
    But hearts to be Thine own.

3. Hosanna! once Thy gracious ear
    Approved a lisping throng;
  Be gracious still, and deign to hear
    Our poor but grateful song.
  O Saviour, if, redeemed by Thee,
    Thy temple we behold,
  Hosannas through eternity
    We'll sing to harps of gold.

331   8, 4.

*" There is a friend that sticketh closer
than a brother."*

1. ONE is kind above all others —
        O how He loves !
His is love beyond a brother's —
        O how He loves !
Earthly friends may fail or leave us,
One day soothe, the next day grieve us :
But this Friend will ne'er deceive us —
        O how he loves !

2. 'Tis eternal life to know Him —
        O how He loves !
Think, O think, how much we owe Him —
        O how He loves !
With His precious blood He bought us,
In the wilderness He sought us,
To His fold He safely brought us —
        O how He loves !

3. Through His name we are forgiven —
        O how He loves !
Backward shall our foes be driven —
        O how He loves !
Best of blessings He'll provide us,
Nought but good shall e'er betide us !
Safe to glory He will guide us —
        O how he loves !

332   7, 6.

" Hosanna to the Son of David."

1. HOSANNA ! loud hosanna
        The little children sang ;
Through pillared court and temple
        The lovely anthem rang ;

288

To Jesus who had blessed them,
   Close folded to His breast,
The children sang their praises,
   The simplest and the best.

2. From Olivet they followed,
   'Midst an exultant crowd,
Waving the victor palm-branch,
   And shouting clear and loud;
Bright angels joined the chorus,
   Beyond the cloudless sky, —
'Hosanna in the highest,
   Glory to God on high!'

3. Fair leaves of silvery olive
   They strewed upon the ground,
Whilst Salem's circling mountains
   Echoed the joyful sound;
The Lord of men and angels
   Rode on in lowly state,
Nor scorned that little children
   Should on His bidding wait.

4. 'Hosanna in the highest!'
   That ancient song we sing;
For Christ is our Redeemer,
   The Lord of heaven our King.
O may we ever praise Him,
   With heart, and life, and voice,
And in his blissful presence
   Eternally rejoice!

333　　　　　　　　　　　　　　　P. M.

" Jesus called a little child unto him."

1. I THINK, when I read that sweet story of old,
   When Jesus was here among men,
How He called little children, as lambs, to His
     fold,
   I should like to have been with Him then.

I wish that His hands had been placed on my
    head,
That His arms had been thrown around me,
And that I might have seen His kind look when
    He said,
  ' Let the little ones come unto Me.'

2. Yet still to His footstool in prayer I may go,
    And ask for a share in His love;
And if I thus earnestly seek Him below,
    I shall see Him and hear Him above,—
In that beautiful place He has gone to prepare
    For all who are washed and forgiven ;
And many dear children are gathering there,
    ' For of such is the kingdom of heaven.'

3. But thousands and thousands who wander and fall
    Never heard of that heavenly home;
I should like them to know there is room for
    them all,
    And that Jesus has bid them to come.
I long for that blessèd and glorious time,
    The fairest and brightest and best,
When the dear little children of every clime
    Shall crowd to His arms and be blest.

334   6, 7.

" The Lord is high, yet hath he respect
to the lowly."

1. JESUS, high in glory,
    Lend a listening ear ;
When we bow before Thee,
    Children's praises hear.

2. Though Thou art so holy,
    Heaven's Almighty King,
Thou wilt stoop to listen
    When Thy praise we sing.

3. We are little children,
    Weak and apt to stray;
  Saviour, guide and keep us
    In the heavenly way.

4. Save us, Lord, from sinning,
    Watch us day by day;
  Help us now to love Thee;
    Take our sins away.

5. Then, when Jesus calls us
    To our heavenly home,
  We would gladly answer,
    'Saviour Lord, we come.'

335   7s.

*" Learn of me, for I am meek and lowly
in heart."*

1. GENTLE Jesus, meek and mild,
    Look upon a little child;
  Pity my simplicity;
    Suffer me to come to Thee.

2. Fain I would to Thee be brought;
    Dearest Lord, forbid it not;
  Give me, dearest Lord, a place
    In the kingdom of Thy grace.

3. Lamb of God, I look to Thee;
    Thou shalt my example be;
  Thou art gentle, meek, and mild,
    Thou wast once a little child.

4. Loving Jesus, gentle Lamb,
    In Thy gracious hands I am;
  Make me, Saviour, what Thou art,
    Live Thyself within my heart.

336

" At thy right hand are pleasures for
evermore."

1. THERE is a happy land,
    Far, far away,
  Where saints in glory stand,
    Bright, bright as day:
  O how they sweetly sing,
  Worthy is our Saviour King!
  Loud let His praises ring,
    Praise, praise for aye.

2. Come to this happy land,
    Come, come away;
  Why will ye doubting stand,
    Why still delay?
  O we shall happy be,
  When from sin and sorrow free,
  Lord, we shall live with Thee,
    Blest, blest for aye.

3. Bright in that happy land
    Beams every eye;
  Kept by a Father's hand,
    Love cannot die:
  On then to glory run;
  Be a crown and kingdom won;
  And, bright above the sun,
    Reign, reign for aye.

337 **8, 7, 6.**

" They shall be mine, saith the Lord of
hosts, in that day when I make up
my jewels."

1. WHEN He cometh, when He cometh,
  To make up His jewels,
  All His jewels, precious jewels,
  His loved and His own,

Like the stars of the morning,
His bright crown adorning,
They shall shine in their beauty,
Bright gems for His crown.

2. He will gather, He will gather,
The gems for His kingdom;
All the pure ones, all the bright ones,
His loved and His own.
Like, &c.

3. Little children, little children,
Who love their Redeemer,
Are the jewels, precious jewels,
His loved and His own.
Like, &c.

338   7, 6.

" In thy presence is fulness of joy."

1. HERE we suffer grief and pain;
Here we meet to part again;
In heaven we part no more.
O that will be joyful,
Joyful, joyful, joyful;
O that will be joyful,
When we meet to part no more.

2. All who love the Lord below,
When they die, to heaven will go,
And sing with saints above.
O that will be joyful,
Joyful, joyful, joyful;
O that will be joyful,
When we meet to part no more.

3. Little children will be there,
Who have sought the Lord by prayer,
From every Sabbath school.

O that will be joyful,
Joyful, joyful, joyful;
O that will be joyful,
When we meet to part no more.

4. O how happy we shall be,
For our Saviour we shall see
Exalted on His throne.
O that will be joyful,
Joyful, joyful, joyful;
O that will be joyful,
When we meet to part no more.

5. There we all shall sing with joy,
And eternity employ
In praising Christ the Lord.
O that will be joyful,
Joyful, joyful, joyful;
O that will be joyful,
When we meet to part no more.

339   **8, 7.**

" Follow me."

1. CHILDHOOD's years are passing o'er us,
Youthful days will soon be done ;
Cares and sorrows lie before us,
Hidden dangers, snares unknown.

2. O may He, who, meek and lowly
Trod Himself this vale of woe,
Make us His, and make us holy,
Guard and guide us while we go.

3. Hark! it is the Saviour calling,
'Little children, follow Me;'
Jesus, keep our feet from falling;
Teach us all to follow Thee.

4. Soon we part — it may be never,
　　Never here to meet again;
O to meet in heaven for ever!
　　O the crown of life to gain!

340　　　　　　　　　8, 7, 4.

1. LORD, dismiss us with Thy blessing,
　　Fill our hearts with joy and peace:
Let us each, Thy love possessing,
　　Triumph in redeeming grace;
　　　O refresh us,
Travelling through life's wilderness!

2. Thanks we give and adoration,
　　For Thy gospel's joyful sound;
May the fruits of Thy salvation
　　In our hearts and lives abound;
　　　May Thy presence
With us evermore be found!

341　　　　　　　　　8s.

1. O SAVIOUR, bless us ere we go;
　　Thy word into our minds instil;
And make our lukewarm hearts to glow
　　With lowly love and fervent will.
Through life's long day and death's dark night,
O gentle Jesus, be our light!

2. The day is gone, its hours have run,
　　And Thou hast taken count of all
The scanty triumphs grace hath won,
　　The broken vow, the frequent fall.
Through life's long day and death's dark night,
O gentle Jesus, be our light!

3. Grant us, O Lord, from evil ways
 True absolution and release ;
And bless us, more than in past days,
 With purity and inward peace.
Through life's long day and death's dark night,
O gentle Jesus, be our light !

4. Labour is sweet, for Thou hast toiled ;
 And care is light, for Thou hast cared ;
Let not our works with self be soiled,
 Nor in unsimple ways ensnared.
Through life's long day and death's dark night,
O gentle Jesus, be our light !

5. Do more than pardon, give us joy,
 Sweet fear, and sober liberty,
And loving hearts without alloy,
 That only long to be like Thee.
Through life's long day and death's dark night,
O gentle Jesus, be our light !

6. For all we love, the poor, the sad,
 The sinful, unto Thee we call ;
O let Thy mercy make us glad !
 Thou art our Jesus and our all.
Through life's long day and death's dark night,
O gentle Jesus, be our light !

342   7s.

1. Now may He who from the dead
 Brought the Shepherd of the sheep,
Jesus Christ, our King and Head,
 All our souls in safety keep.

2. May He teach us to fulfil
 What is pleasing in His sight,

Perfect us in all His will,
And preserve us day and night.

3. To that great Redeemer's praise,
Who the covenant sealed with blood,
Let our hearts and voices raise
Loud thanksgivings to our God.

343   8, 7.

1. MAY the grace of Christ our Saviour,
And the Father's boundless love,
With the Holy Spirit's favour,
Rest upon us from above.

2. Thus may we abide in union
With each other and the Lord,
And possess in sweet communion,
Joys which earth cannot afford.

344   8, 7.

1. LORD, dismiss us with Thy blessing,
Bid us now depart in peace;
Still on heavenly manna feeding,
Let our faith and love increase:
Fill each breast with consolation;
Up to Thee our hearts we raise:
When we reach yon blissful station,
Then we'll give Thee nobler praise.
Hallelujah!

345   L. M.

1. FROM all that dwell below the skies
Let the Creator's praise arise;
Let the Redeemer's name be sung
Through every land, by every tongue.

2. Eternal are Thy mercies, Lord,
Eternal truth attends Thy word.
Thy praise shall sound from shore to shore,
Till suns shall rise and set no more.

346 L. M.

DISMISS us with Thy blessing, Lord;
Help us to feed upon Thy word;
All that has been amiss forgive,
And let Thy truth within us live.
Though we are guilty Thou art good,
Sprinkle our works with Jesus' blood;
Give every fettered soul release,
And bid us all depart in peace.

347 7S.

PART in peace! Christ's life was peace,
   Let us live our life in Him;
Part in peace! Christ's death was peace,
   Let us die our death in Him:
Part in peace! Christ promise gave
Of a life beyond the grave,
Where all mortal partings cease;
Brethren, sisters, part in peace.

348

WE praise Thee, O God: we acknowledge Thee
to be the Lord.
All the earth doth worship Thee: the Father
everlasting.
To Thee all angels cry aloud: the heavens, and
all the powers therein.
To Thee cherubim and seraphim continually do
cry,

Holy, holy, holy: Lord God of Sabaoth;
Heaven and earth are full of the majesty: of
Thy glory.
The glorious company of the apostles: praise
Thee.
The goodly fellowship of the prophets: praise
Thee.
The noble army of martyrs: praise Thee.
The holy Church throughout all the world: doth
acknowledge Thee;
The Father: of an infinite majesty;
Thine honourable, true: and only Son;
Also the Holy Ghost: the Comforter.
Thou art the King of glory: O Christ.
Thou art the everlasting Son: of the Father.
When Thou tookest upon Thee to deliver man:
Thou didst not abhor the Virgin's womb.
When Thou hadst overcome the sharpness of
death: Thou didst open the kingdom of heaven to
all believers.
Thou sittest at the right hand of God: in the
glory of the Father.
We believe that Thou shalt come: to be our
Judge.
We therefore pray Thee, help Thy servants:
whom Thou hast redeemed with Thy precious
blood.
Make them to be numbered with Thy saints: in
glory everlasting.
O Lord, save Thy people: and bless Thine heri-
tage.
Govern them: and lift them up for ever.
Day by day: we magnify Thee;
And we worship Thy name: ever world without
end.
Vouchsafe, O Lord: to keep us this day without
sin.
O Lord, have mercy upon us: have mercy upon
us.

O Lord, let Thy mercy lighten upon us: as our trust is in Thee.

O Lord, in Thee have I trusted: let me never be confounded.

349

GLORY be to God on high, and on earth peace, good-will toward men.

WE praise Thee, we bless Thee, we worship Thee, we glorify Thee, we give thanks to Thee for Thy great glory,

O LORD God, heavenly King, God the Father Almighty.

O LORD, the only begotten Son, Jesus Christ: O Lord God, Lamb of God, Son of the Father,

THAT takest away the sins of the world, have mercy upon us.

THOU that takest away the sins of the world, have mercy upon us.

THOU that takest away the sins of the world, receive our prayer.

THOU that sittest at the right hand of God the Father, have mercy upon us.

FOR Thou only art holy; Thou only art the Lord;

THOU only, O Christ, with the Holy Ghost, art most high in the glory of God the Father. Amen.

DOXOLOGIES.

1

BLESSÈD, blessèd be Jehovah,
  Israel's God, to all eternity:
Let all the people say, Amen.
  Amen. Praise to the Lord give ye.

2

GLORY be to the Father, and to the Son: and to
  the Holy Ghost;
As it was in the beginning, is now, and ever shall
  be; world without end. Amen.

3   8s.

IMMORTAL honour, endless fame
Attend the Almighty Father's name!
Let God the Son be glorified,
Who for lost man's redemption died!
And equal adoration be,
Eternal Spirit, paid to Thee!

4   C. M.

Now blessèd be the Lord our God,
  the God of Israel,
For He alone doth wondrous works,
  in glory that excel.

301

And blessed be His glorious name
  to all eternity:
The whole earth let His glory fill.
  Amen, so let it be.

5   **8, 7, 4.**

Now to Him who loved us, gave us
  Every pledge that love could give,
Freely shed His blood to save us,
  Gave His life that we might live:
      Be the kingdom
      And dominion,
And the glory, evermore.

6   **L. M.**

PRAISE God from whom all blessings flow:
Praise Him, all creatures here below;
Praise Him above, ye heavenly host;
Praise Father, Son, and Holy Ghost.

7   **C. M.**

SALVATION and immortal praise
  To our victorious King!
Let heaven and earth, and rocks and seas,
  With glad hosannas ring.

To Father, Son, and Holy Ghost,
  The God whom we adore,
Be glory, as it was, and is,
  And shall be evermore.

8   L. M.

To God the Father, God the Son,
And God the Spirit, Three in One,
Be honour, praise, and glory given,
By all on earth and all in heaven.

9   C. M.

To Him that loved the souls of men,
    And washed us in His blood,
To royal honours raised our head,
    And made us priests to God;—

To Him let every tongue be praise,
    And every heart be love!
All grateful honours paid on earth,
    And nobler songs above!

10

HOLY, holy, holy: Lord God of Hosts!
Heaven and earth are full of the majesty of Thy
        glory;
Glory be to Thee, O Lord Most High.

11

LORD, bless us still!
            O bless us still!
Lord, hear our prayers!
            O hear our prayers!
Accept our praise!
            Accept our praise!
Hallelujah!
            Praised be Thy holy name! Amen.

12

HALLELUJAH! for the Lord God omnipotent
    reigneth.
The kingdoms of this world are become the king-
    doms of our Lord and of His Christ;
And He shall reign for ever and ever;
King of Kings and Lord of Lords: Hallelujah!

13   6, 4.

Now to the King of Heaven
  Your cheerful voices raise;
To Him be glory given,
  Power, majesty and praise;
    Wide as He reigns,
      His name be sung
      By every tongue,
    In endless strains.

INDEX OF FIRST LINES.

311

INDEX OF FIRST LINES.

DOXOLOGIES.

INDEX OF FIRST LINES

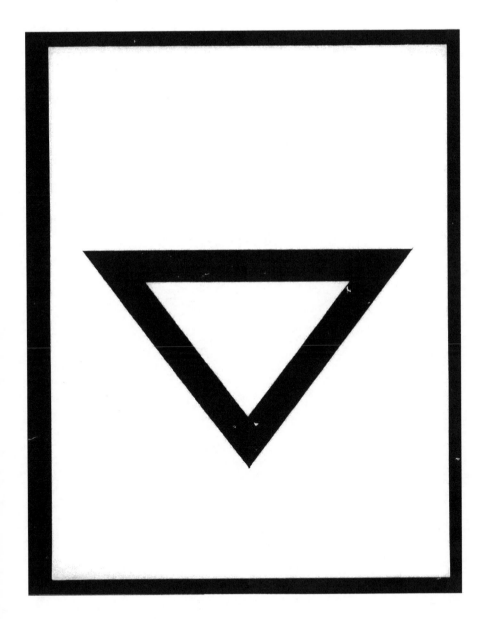